Developing AR Games for iOS and Android

Develop and deploy augmented reality apps using Vuforia SDK and Unity 3D

Dominic Cushnan

Hassan El Habbak

PUBLISHING

BIRMINGHAM - MUMBAI

Developing AR Games for iOS and Android

First published: September 2013

Production Reference: 1170913

Published by Packt Publishing Ltd.
Livery Place
35 Livery Street
Birmingham B3 2PB, UK..

ISBN 978-1-78328-003-2

www.packtpub.com

Cover Image by Dominic Cushnan (dominic@mixedrealitystudio.com)

Credits

Authors

Dominic Cushnan

Hassan El Habbak

Reviewers

Thomas Finnegan

Nguyen Duc Luong

Acquisition Editor

James Jones

Commissioning Editor

Mohammed Fahad

Technical Editors

Krutika Parab

Gaurav Thingalaya

Dennis John

Project Coordinator

Joel Goveya

Proofreaders

Stephen Copestake

Clyde Jenkins

Indexer

Rekha Nair

Production Coordinator

Shantanu Zagade

Cover Work

Shantanu Zagade

About the Authors

Dominic Cushnan is a visionary, and he is always looking for the next new idea and technology to analyze. He is currently the director of a software company dedicated to bringing augmented reality solutions to various types of clients in various fields. Dominic began developing web-based AR projects, and he has seen the industry grow and develop over the years. Working initially with advertising agencies and brands, Dominic is excited to see the consumer AR market expand.

> I would like to thank all the support I have had from mentors to clients and friends who share my vision and the ever patient "squirrel". Mostly I would like to thank Hassan for being a great team player and true friend.

Hassan EL Habbak is a software engineer with a huge interest in mobile technologies, particularly in the areas of AR and gaming. He started off with small-scale mobile applications, but soon found himself creating massive AR experiences for a variety of businesses and individuals. He is also a gaming enthusiast with various games already implemented using free technologies such as Unity. He thrives on finding channels through which he may deliver his content to the masses of unsuspecting people.

> I would like to thank my wife, without whom none of this would have happened. I would like to thank Dominic for being the friend that supported me for years now. I would like to thank everyone who has ever worked or improved tech; we stand on shoulders of giants.

About the Reviewers

Thomas Finnegan graduated from Brown College in 2010, and now works as a freelance game developer. Since then, he has worked on everything from mobile platforms to web development, and even experimental devices. Past clients include Carmichael Lynch, Coleco, and Subaru. His most recent project is Battle Box 3D, a virtual table top. His first book, about Android Game Development in Unity 3D, will see release in early 2014.

Nguyen Duc Luong has two diplomas, one in Information Technology, and one for Business Administration; with him study is good. He has started as Software Engineer, but he has experience of more than seven years as a developer. With passion in programming, he has developed a lot of complex and distributed system on desktop, web base for government and business organizations projects, in many programming languages. He also has strong experience in developing apps and games on smartphones (iOS and Android OS) in the century of mobile. Recent languages that he focuses on now are Ruby, C++, C#, Objective-C, with some game engines such as Cocos2d and Unity, and some frameworks for app on mobile such as jQuery Mobile and PhoneGap.

www.PacktPub.com

Support files, eBooks, discount offers and more

You might want to visit www.PacktPub.com for support files and downloads related to your book.

Did you know that Packt offers eBook versions of every book published, with PDF and ePub files available? You can upgrade to the eBook version at www.PacktPub.com and as a print book customer, you are entitled to a discount on the eBook copy. Get in touch with us at service@packtpub.com for more details.

At www.PacktPub.com, you can also read a collection of free technical articles, sign up for a range of free newsletters and receive exclusive discounts and offers on Packt books and eBooks.

http://PacktLib.PacktPub.com

Do you need instant solutions to your IT questions? PacktLib is Packt's online digital book library. Here, you can access, read and search across Packt's entire library of books.

Why Subscribe?

- Fully searchable across every book published by Packt
- Copy and paste, print and bookmark content
- On demand and accessible via web browser

Free Access for Packt account holders

If you have an account with Packt at www.PacktPub.com, you can use this to access PacktLib today and view nine entirely free books. Simply use your login credentials for immediate access.

Table of Contents

Preface

In this book, we will be introduced to augmented reality, and how to achieve it using powerful but simple tools. Using the free license of Vuforia and Unity 3D, we will see how the two technologies can seamlessly entwine and produce amazing results. We will learn how to design a great augmented reality experience that will immerse users and not feel foreign when augmented on the real world. Augmented reality became increasingly reliable with recent advancements in the field; we will learn how to use that potential in most efficient way.

What this book covers

Chapter 1, *What is Augmented Reality?*, will explain what is augmented reality, and what is its past, present, and future.

Chapter 2, *Setting Up the Environment*, will cover how to set up the environment necessary for AR using Unity 3D and Vuforia, and also how to deploy AR on iOS and Android devices.

Chapter 3, *Understanding Vuforia*, will go through the components of Vuforia and how they work together to achieve augmented reality.

Chapter 4, *Trackables and Tracking*, will explain how to create trackables for Vuforia and how to optimize them to achieve highest tracking scores.

Chapter 5, *Advanced Augmented Reality*, will introduce how to make fully-functional AR games using Unity and Vuforia.

What you need for this book

The free version of Unity 3D is required, as well as Vuforia SDK.

Who this book is for

This book is for anyone with basic to advanced programming experience, who is interested in AR and game development. In a booming smartphones industry, this book is for anyone looking for entry into the immersive mobile experience using interactive games and AR.

Conventions

In this book, you will find a number of styles of text that distinguish among different kinds of information. Here are some examples of these styles, and an explanation of their meaning.

Code words in text are shown as follows: "We can include other contexts through the use of the include directive."

New terms and **important words** are shown in bold. Words that you see on the screen, in menus or dialog boxes for example, appear in the text like this: "clicking the **Next** button moves you to the next screen".

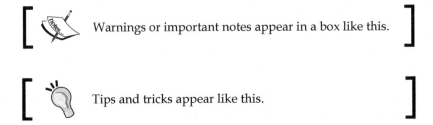

Warnings or important notes appear in a box like this.

Tips and tricks appear like this.

Reader feedback

Feedback from our readers is always welcome. Let us know what you think about this book—what you liked or may have disliked. Reader feedback is important for us to develop titles that you really get the most out of.

To send us general feedback, simply send an e-mail to feedback@packtpub.com, and mention the book title via the subject of your message.

If there is a topic that you have expertise in and you are interested in either writing or contributing to a book, see our author guide on www.packtpub.com/authors.

Customer support

Now that you are the proud owner of a Packt book, we have a number of things to help you to get the most from your purchase.

Downloading the example code

You can download the example code files for all Packt books you have purchased from your account at http://www.packtpub.com. If you purchased this book elsewhere, you can visit http://www.packtpub.com/support and register to have the files e-mailed directly to you.

Errata

Although we have taken every care to ensure the accuracy of our content, mistakes do happen. If you find a mistake in one of our books—maybe a mistake in the text or the code—we would be grateful if you would report this to us. By doing so, you can save other readers from frustration and help us improve subsequent versions of this book. If you find any errata, please report them by visiting http://www.packtpub.com/submit-errata, selecting your book, clicking on the **errata submission form** link, and entering the details of your errata. Once your errata are verified, your submission will be accepted and the errata will be uploaded on our website, or added to any list of existing errata, under the Errata section of that title. Any existing errata can be viewed by selecting your title from http://www.packtpub.com/support.

Piracy

Piracy of copyright material on the Internet is an ongoing problem across all media. At Packt, we take the protection of our copyright and licenses very seriously. If you come across any illegal copies of our works, in any form, on the Internet, please provide us with the location address or website name immediately so that we can pursue a remedy.

Please contact us at copyright@packtpub.com with a link to the suspected pirated material.

We appreciate your help in protecting our authors, and our ability to bring you valuable content.

Questions

You can contact us at questions@packtpub.com if you are having a problem with any aspect of the book, and we will do our best to address it.

1
What is Augmented Reality?

In augmented reality, the reality around us is layered on with virtual content. Whether that is an immersive 3D experience or simple text and indicators, virtual reality is both an old concept and a rising new technology. In this chapter we will go over the concept of augmented reality in its many forms, to broaden our view of the scope of the concept and how it can be utilized. We will also go over the tools that will help us materialize this concept in the explosively growing mobile platforms, particularly iOS devices. The following image shows an augmented reality game:

Definition of augmented reality

Augmented reality (AR) in its broadest and simplest definition is the technology that enables the addition of virtual content to the real world. This is usually associated with the addition of 3D content to a live feed from camera, though the term in itself has a much broader meaning and usage.

Perhaps the simplest form of augmented reality that people have been using for decades is the one available in photo cameras more than a decade ago. Many use it, but very few realized the nature of the concept applied. It's the part of the camera called "the viewfinder", which is the little window you look through to view the world through the camera. This little window is in fact an augmented reality in a very simple form. What it fundamentally does is look at the world around it through the lens and then add a layer printed on glass to highlight the center of the lens and the borders of the image to be captured. What it did here is what augmented reality in all its forms aspires to do, which is to layer relative information over the real world.

In mobile platforms, augmented reality works on the same principles even if the method is slightly different. The camera captures a live feed of the world around it, and then the computer vision systems try to get a bearing in the visible 3D space and display the augmented reality in a way that is seamless with the world. The process of calculating the relative position of the user to the reality around, to be able to correctly augment the content for the user, is called tracking.

The forms of augmented reality

Augmented reality can take many forms. It always depends in one form or another on a technique to calculate the relative 3D space to the reality around us. It can achieve that using many technologies. For example, the Gyroscope on an iPhone can be used to track the placement of the phone in the 3D space that can be used to track the world relative to the device if movement is applied. That is usually seen in a number of augmented reality games for the device. That is certainly a form of AR but in this book, we will be mainly concerned with one form of tracking that uses computer vision.

Computer vision tracking can be divided into two sections, marker tracking and markerless tracking. In marker tracking, there is a physical entity that the computer vision is trained to track; it positions the camera's perspective relative to it. The physical object used is usually called a trackable. The trackable is usually handled internally to be the origin and the center of the world, which the computer vision can orient itself to. Sometimes, the camera live feed is the one considered to be the center of the world, and the trackable or trackables are objects that orbit it in space so to speak.

Markerless tracking techniques are essentially similar to marker tracking in that they try to find an origin point to augment the reality relative to. They differ in the way they find the origin point that, unlike marker tracking, they achieve without using a predefined physical object that the computer vision is only trained to follow. In Markerless tracking, the computer vision is mainly programmed to follow certain colors and shapes with a degree of freedom. For example, the computer can be trained to follow green objects of a certain shade and cover them completely with a blue one. In this case, it simply tracks the color; if it finds a green area in the camera feed, it augments it with a blue virtual object. Computer vision can even be trained to recognize faces, such as all the famous camera apps that add animated effects around the user's head or face. Markerless tracking is definitely more versatile, but it offers less reliability than marker tracking. Also Markerless tracking is naturally more complicated to develop, contributing to the popularity of the Marker tracking augmented reality.

In this book, we will use the Vuforia SDK, which is an SDK that uses Marker tracking techniques. We will use this with the Unity 3D engine to deliver augmented reality experiences on iOS devices. In utilizing both technologies, we will be familiarizing ourselves with the workflow of creating augmented reality.

Smartphones and augmented reality

As we have established, the concept of augmented reality is an old one. It is even woven into the pop-culture in sci-fi movies as old as we can remember. Augmented reality as a technology did not reach the mainstream till quite recently. In the past, augmented reality was considered a niche, because of the expensive setup it needed to function. Augmented reality is demanding when it comes to hardware. It needs a camera to view the world with, computational power to calculate and render the augmented content, and a way for the user to interact with the virtual content. All of this was difficult to attain for mainstream users.

Today, almost everyone is walking around with very capable computers in their pockets able to render graphics content to a large degree of realism. Those smartphones are evolving at an unprecedented pace that makes them more and more powerful by the month. And best of all, they come with an accurate camera, fulfilling all the three needs for augmented reality.

It is not very inaccurate to assume that everyone is walking around with an augmented reality-capable machine at his or her will. That alone eradicated the barrier to accessibility that was present for so long. Now augmented reality content can reach millions of users for an unprecedented immersive experience.

A lot of companies understood the importance of the trend in the industry and its potential. Perhaps in the lead is Qualcomm, the biggest mobile chip manufacturer in the world. Qualcomm realized the huge potential of AR present in mobile phones, and developed the free SDK Vuforia. Vuforia, known as QCAR in the past, was created to enable developers to tap that potential in the mobile space. Vuforia started out on Android platforms, and later expanded to include iOS devices as well. Qualcomm always includes subtle optimizations to AR on their chips to further improve the experience. This shows how much they believe in the future of the technology. Qualcomm even invested in making a more mobile-friendly OpenCV SDK called Easy CV. Easy CV is a tool for image processing and computer vision that can further enhance the experience of AR along other uses that involve computer vision.

Google also is heavily invested in the concept of augmented reality with their Google Glass project. Google Glass is perhaps the most ambitious augmented reality project under development right now. It promises wearable computers for the mainstream in the form of a head mounted display equipped with a camera. The design is to be unobtrusive, but at the same time efficient at displaying augmented reality data based on the input of the real world. Interaction will be in the form of voice commands and it will be able to access the Internet. The project is still in its infancy but the fact that Google is investing so many resources, clearly indicates the importance of the rising AR technology.

With the accessibility of augmented reality hardware, the support of major corporations, and the huge market available, augmented reality has everything it needs to thrive and stay for a long time. This is why it is important to familiarize us with the concept and its potential.

Immersion factor for delivering content

Immersion is the factor in which the user is engrossed in the world you presented to them. The more believable the world, the more immersed the user will be, and the more successful the message the experience is trying to convey. The successful developer will try to achieve the highest level of immersion possible.

The human mind will always try to make sense of what it's seeing; that is true for all human interactions. This fact is particularly interesting for virtual interaction because what the human mind is trying to make sense of is not physically there. The more elaborate the lie, the easier the mind will believe it. So the art of immersion is the art of telling the perfect lie to the mind. And as all good liars will say, if they were honest for that moment, the way to tell the perfect lie is to mix it with the truth. By that definition, augmented reality is the perfect way of telling a lie.

By mixing the virtual content with the real world, the user feels connected to the content presented in a way most other virtual medias fall short of. Watching a user interact with augmented reality content for the first time is always wonderful. Often, we can see that the user forgets for a moment that they are watching the virtual content through the screen of their device and try to grab it with their hands as if to check it's not really there. It happens almost consistently and certainly subconsciously. This is indicative of how much the user is immersed in the action.

What adds to the immersion as well is the way the user can interact with the augmented reality content. The user can view the content from almost all angles. They can walk around it, come close to it, and walk away from it. The fact that it stays consistent with the world around them, maintains the connection between the user and the content. If the experience is mixed with the right audio and/or video content, it can be something that brings a smile on the user's face.

Interactivity can even come in the form of a game structure that allows the user to directly affect the content being displayed. Interactivity of this kind can be very entertaining for the user and a fresh way of playing a game.

Vuforia SDK and how it helps in delivering the AR experience

Vuforia is a great offering from Qualcomm that gave the augmented reality industry a great boost. It has one of the fastest tracking algorithms in the market that is less prone to trackable occlusion and even low light conditions. This makes the apps created using the SDK user-friendly and easy to use. Best of all, the Vuforia SDK is offered for free, making it widely used with an active community on the forums tackling most issues that might arise.

The SDK is also particularly friendly to developers new to the concept. It is easy to learn with a smooth workflow that just makes sense. Using this SDK will allow developers to deploy simple AR apps in very little time, and still allows them to develop robust and complex AR experiences.

Vuforia offers easy to use components that perform the augmented reality role when interacting together. For example, the SDK offers the ARCamera component. The ARCamera component will automatically take the video camera feed from the device and display it for the use. It will also detect trackables that the developer specified for the camera. The ARCamera will respond to the orientation of the user in relation to the trackable mostly without much intervention from the developer. This simplifies the process of creating an augmented reality experience greatly.

Vuforia also offers a number of tracking solutions that cover a number of situations. The list of components offered in the SDK is as follows:

- **ARCamera**: This is essentially the user's portal into the real world through the app. It offers the live camera feed from the device and also the number of trackables to detect.

- **Image Target**: This is the most common form of trackables offered by Vuforia. Using this component, the app can detect any suitable image it has been trained to detect and show the AR content layered on top of it. By simply adding the content to this component and setting what image it needs to track, the AR content will appear relative to the trackable image in the real world. The following image shows Image Target with a 3D object rendered:

- **Frame Marker**: This is a square marker with code embedded around its internal edges. There are 100 coded Frame Markers that Vuforia offers for you that the app can detect using their coded number and display AR content on top of them. Frame Markers can be smaller than Image Targets, and we can add any sort of image inside their borders without having to worry about how well they can be tracked. It's suitable for game pieces or playing cards. With a minimal performance hit, many of them can be tracked simultaneously at the same time. The following image shows a Frame Marker image:

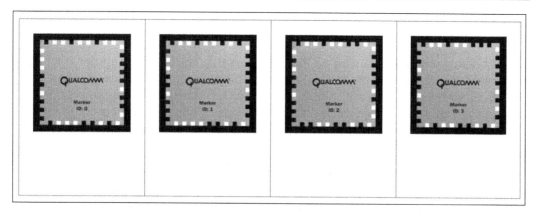

- **Multi-Targets**: Multi-Targets allow developers to track a simple physical box from any angle. The box must have suitably detailed images on it, and must be of a simple shape. Using Multi-Targets can even allow occlusion of AR content from the physical object. It means that if an object is to rotate around the box being tracked, it can be developed so that the 3D is occluded when it passes behind the object being tracked.

- **Virtual Button**: Virtual Button is an interesting technology that can add to the whole AR experience. What this component does is allow the user to touch a physical part of the trackable image, and the app will respond to it. There can be more than one Virtual Button on the Image Target and all can be assigned different events. The following screenshot shows a Virtual Button affecting the color of a rendered object:

With the array of options Vuforia provides, a complete and rich AR experience can be achieved on the powerful smartphones most have with them right now.

In this book, we will be focusing on the most versatile and widely popular tracking technology that is Image Target. Using Image Targets, a natural experience can be delivered to the user because of how relevant the trackable image can be. For example, the trackable image can be an advertisement with information on it but also, if looked at through the AR app, it displays a video playback layered on the image as if the image came to life.

The tracking data of Image Targets are stored in entities called datasets. In datasets, the data of the image such as the edges and contrasting areas are stored, and the ARCamera keeps on processing the live feed video looking for areas that match any of the images inside the dataset. When that happens, the trackable is considered found in the real world and AR content is layered on. The app can have more than one dataset active simultaneously. Each dataset can have up to 100 images. That is a lot of data the app can process in real-time, which shows how powerful Vuforia can be.

The Image Target creation process is also a simple one using Vuforia **Target Manager**, which can create datasets from images, and even assign a score of how well that particular image can be tracked. The trackability of the image depends on many factors, mainly high contrast and well-defined edges. The following image shows the Vuforia **Target Manager** website:

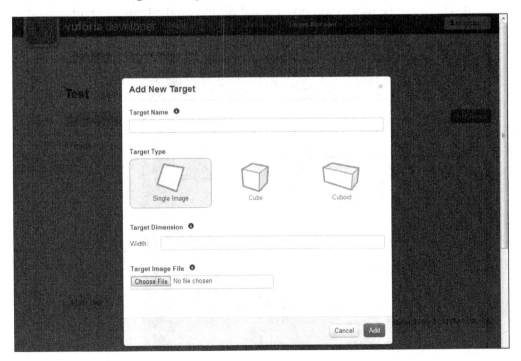

Vuforia also offers a number of solutions for Image Target behavior. One of the services it offers is cloud-based recognition. The Cloud Recognition service provided by Qualcomm enables apps to have over one million Image Targets at the same time. It allows an easier management of a large number of targets as well. This service is well suited for large deployment of targets that are subject to change, such as for retail stores to create an AR shopping experience. The service is free but limited to 1000 total images for non-business use and paid but unlimited for business.

Also Vuforia allows the user to create a user-defined Image Target at runtime from a camera shot. This is a great versatile tool that doesn't tie the user to a specific target image that might not always be available for the user every time the app is needed. The following image shows User-defined Target sample app from Vuforia:

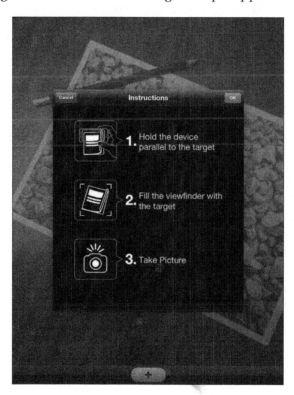

There are many ways we can use the great tools provided in the SDK. We will try to cover the basics that will allow the creation of a well-defined AR experience that will resonate with the user.

Unity 3D and how it fits with Vuforia

Unity is a cross-platform game engine that is developed by Unity Technologies. The game engine has a built in IDE and the ability to deploy to numerous platforms. More than one million developers, making it the most popular game engine in the industry to date, are using Unity. It is designed for ease of use and high productivity. And because of its relatively easy learning curve and the fact that there is a free version of it being offered, encouraged some schools to teach Unity as an introduction to game development.

Unity's greatest strength is its ability to deploy on a large number of platforms with ease and few changes to the project's structure. Unity's name comes from that particular strength. Unity can deploy on Windows, OS X, iOS, Android, Web plugin, Flash, Xbox 360, PlayStation 3, and Wii U. That kind of reach opens up a lot of opportunities when developing using Unity engine.

Unity allows you to choose from three languages to write scripts with. The languages available are JavaScript, C#, or Boo. Unity ships with a customized version of MonoDevelop for debugging purposes. In the same project, a combination of scripts using any of these languages is allowable, though it is recommended to only use one scripting language throughout the entire project to avoid any conflicts and to be easier to read and understand. In this book, we will use C# as the scripting language. The reason for the choice is that Vuforia uses C# for its scripts, and that makes it easier to communicate with Vuforia scripts as we will see later on. Also C# is a well-structured language that, while having a higher learning curve than JavaScript, is much more robust and less prone to mistakes. It is the language of choice for most professional studios as well. The following screenshot shows Unity project window:

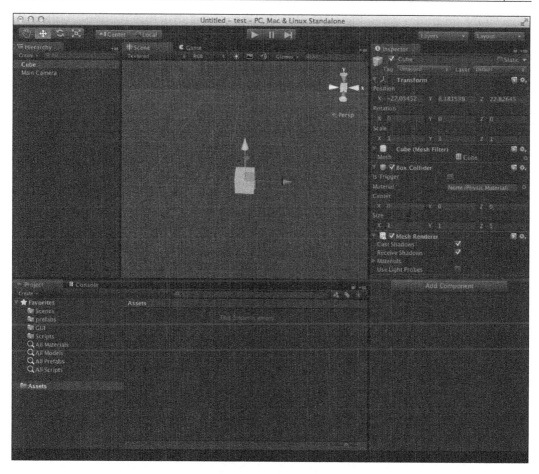

The preceding screenshot can be intimidating for the uninitiated, but through this book we will go over a lot of the basics of Unity engine. In the book we will go over how to create a new project and the deployment process needed to deploy on IOS devices. We will also cover some game development techniques by making our simple AR game and establish how the user can interact with the AR content.

Though Vuforia offers an OpenGL SDK that we can use to create AR apps natively without having to use Unity, Unity offers a lot of tools that would simply take too long to create using OpenGL. Unity is a game engine that offers a lot of tools that can make 3D content look incredibly good and realistic. Some of the best-looking iPhone and iPad games on the iTunes market are created using Unity engine. Some of these games are Dead Trigger and Shadowgun, both incredibly good-looking games on the platform.

Also Unity simplifies game logic greatly with the robust structure it offers. It offers a window into how the 3D graphics will look exactly and even how interactions will look. Unity using Vuforia can utilize a webcam to detect trackables and even show you how exactly the AR content will be on the trackable without having to deploy on the device first. That saves a lot of time that could have been wasted simply deploying on devices to find out that the 3D content doesn't look or behave correctly on the trackable.

Lately Unity opened up their license options to allow anyone to deploy to iOS and Android for free. We do not need to buy their license to be able to deploy simple Vuforia apps. Although Unity pro does offer many strong features, they are not necessary in the course of our book.

Summary

In this chapter we were introduced to the meaning and possibilities of augmented reality. It is a very exciting field that has been briefly introduced in this chapter. We have been introduced to the many forms of augmented reality and how it manifested themselves in the hand of the users in the form of smartphones. We know also understand how powerful AR is at delivering immersive experience for users.

We were introduced to Vuforia, the free AR SDK by Qualcomm. We understand how powerful it can be in improving the flow of creating AR apps for users. Having it handle the technicalities of AR and allowing us to focus on making a better experience. We know the many tracking techniques that Vuforia offers and how different of an experience each can deliver. This should allow us to better utilize them in the future.

Unity was introduced to us, we have a vague idea of how powerful that engine is or how it can enable us as developers to forge AR experience as creatively as we want them. In the book, we will further explore the surface of Unity's power. While we won't be able to go through everything that is Unity in this book, we will see how simple knowledge in a few components can create impressive AR apps.

In the next chapter, we will go through the process of setting up our environment to start creating AR apps. We will set up both Unity and Vuforia to better understand how they both work together. We will also deploy Vuforia sample apps on device to test how a final app looks like.

2
Setting Up the Environment

In this chapter, we will go over setting up the environment we need for augmented reality, and also deploy our first working augmented reality app. We will get a feel for how the end products feel and how to deploy them. The chapter will lightly touch areas such as Unity platform settings and Vuforia prefabs. The chapter, however, will not cover iOS Apple provisioning and Xcode management since they are outside the scope of the book.

Downloading and installing Unity 3D

The process of downloading and installing Unity on Mac OS X is quite simple. Simply by going to its website and downloading the free trial version of iOS and Android, we can get most of Unity's power instantly for free for a limited time. To download, use the following link: `http://unity3d.com/unity/download/`. Notice that iOS can only be deployed on Mac OS X.

The following image shows the Unity website with free trial:

Once Unity is downloaded, installation is quite straightforward. We can choose the trial version to try out Unity Pro with increased features. The free version will still allow us to deploy to both Android and iOS, but Pro features includes shaders and playing video files. For more information on what is included in the Pro version, check Unity's website.

Downloading and installing Vuforia

Vuforia made a lot of effort to simplify the installation process of the SDK and streamline its workflow so as not to be intimidating to new developers. We will go over the process of installing Vuforia SDK on Mac OS X in preparation of deploying our first augmented reality app.

Vuforia offers a number of different SDK versions that might seem confusing at first; so we will go over them:

- Android native SDK which is to be used with Eclipse and Ant to deploy on android devices, without the need for Unity
- iOS native SDK that is used to deploy on iOS devices using Xcode without the need for Unity
- Unity extension for Android and iOS that is used to deploy on either Android or iOS using Unity's cross-platform capabilities

What we will cover in the book is Vuforia Unity's extension. To download it, please go to the following link:

```
https://developer.vuforia.com/resources/sdk/unity
```

There is a simple registration process before being able to download the SDKs. The following screenshot shows Vuforia SDK Unity extension:

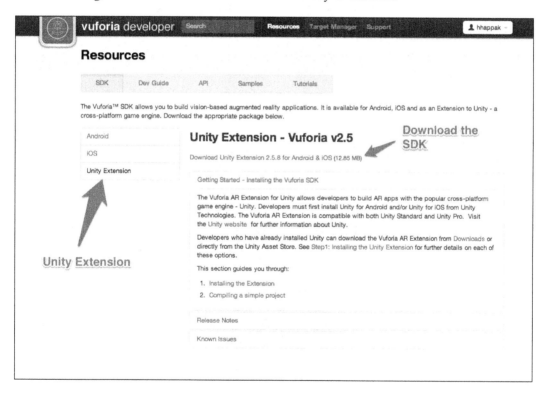

The download file is a Unity package file that, as we will see soon, is very easy to add to a Unity project. There are no further files needed for the SDK. With this, we have everything we need to start developing AR apps on iOS. Unity, the game engine that will facilitate rendering of 3D objects and game logic for us, Vuforia will provide the augmented reality components and Xcode will finally deploy the app on the device.

Vuforia sample projects

Vuforia offers a rather colorful sample project for every SDK version they have for users to see how the SDK can be used. We will utilize those sample projects to be an entry point for us to see how the structure of a finished Vuforia project looks and how to deploy it on iOS and Android devices.

Vuforia offers their sample projects as a package. This package contains a number of applications for Vuforia SDK, but we will focus on Image Target in this book. Let's download the sample projects from the following link `https://developer.vuforia.com/resources/sample-apps`.

The following screenshot shows Vuforia sample apps:

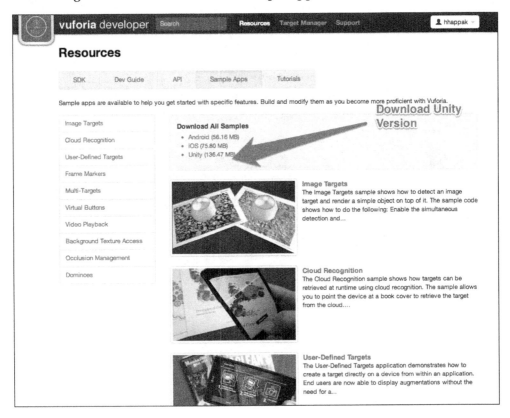

After downloading the compressed project samples, decompress the folder and take a look inside it. The folder will contain a number of files called packages. Those are essentially Unity files that can be imported inside unity projects with ease.

Starting a Unity project

Now that we have downloaded everything that we need, it's time to start a Unity project. Launch Unity, and from the **File** menu, select a new project. Place the project anywhere you would like, but make sure the project name does not have any spaces to avoid later problems. You will be greeted with the Unity's project window. It may seem intimidating a little and feels foreign if this is the first time with a game engine, but we will familiarize ourselves with it as we build our project. The following screenshot shows the Unity project window.

Unity scenes

The following screenshot shows Unity scenes:

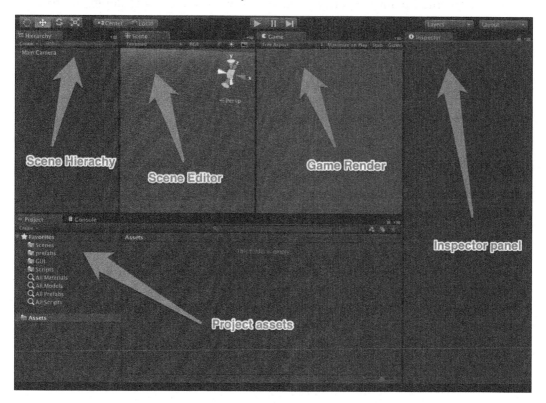

The first concept we will familiarize ourselves with is the scene. The scene is primarily the game level that everything is built inside. It is what is loaded and presented to the user on runtime. It contains all of the game objects such as menus and 3D models. It is the world that we are creating for the user. We can have multiple scenes just as a game has multiple levels.

The **Hierarchy (Scene Hierarchy)** as shown in the preceding screenshot represents the objects in the scene and their relationship between each other. For example, a cube object could be the parent of a sphere object; that way whenever the cube object moves, the sphere object will follow it. This is particularly useful for constructing complex objects such as a car, for example, and has the car parts move with the parent rather than individually. This concept is really important and fundamental to how Vuforia works in Unity.

The **Game (Game Render)** window is a rather useful tool in Unity. It gives a preview of how the game works and looks without the need for deployment, saving a lot of time. Any changes in script or in **Scene (Scene Editor)** will show right away when the play button at the top is clicked and the game "runs". This will allow us to see how the augmented reality experience plays out without having to deploy on the device first.

The **Project (Project assets)** panel is where all of the project assets are. This is where models and textures are imported to the project and even Vuforia SDK. This is also where all the scripts are stored for the app. It is always crucial to keep the assets folder organized and following a certain convention. Projects can grow bigger and keeping track of where assets are can prove very difficult if a project assets hierarchy is not followed.

Inspector (Inspector panel) is where components and assets are tweaked. It displays all the settings for the currently selected scene object from the project hierarchy or assets from the **Project (Project assets)** panel. The inspector is a versatile tool that is used extensively while building a project.

Now that Unity's GUI has been demystified, we can take a look at the sample projects folder we have downloaded from Vuforia. It will contain a number of package files with the name of the project they represent. Package files are very important for Unity. The need to transfer assets from one project to another is not uncommon in game development. Often projects share common assets between them, so Unity needed an efficient way of transferring assets between projects. That's why Unity package files came to be.

In Unity, it is possible to select certain files from the asset store, and even entire scenes, to be exported as a package file. Sometimes the entire project can be exported as a package file. Later that file can be imported into a Unity project and become usable right away.

Vuforia sample projects are in the form of Unity packages, which must be imported into a Unity project to be able to deploy those projects. It is useful to mention that even Vuforia's SDK is offered in the form of a Unity package that can be imported into any project and can utilize its AR components.

Importing packages in Unity

Now we import the sample project into the Unity project that we have created. The following screenshot shows Unity importing `ImageTarget` sample project:

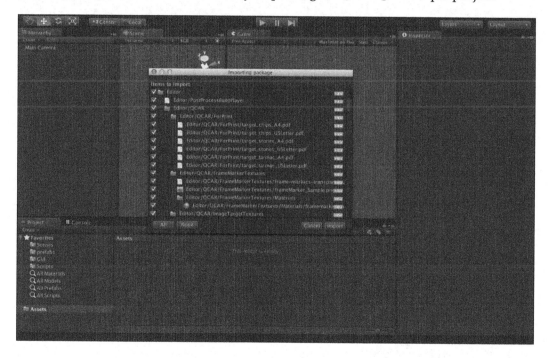

Importing packages is quite a simple process. Go to the **Assets** menu on the top and choose import packaged, and then choose the custom package. Navigate to where Vuforia's sample projects are and choose the image target file. A window like the previous screenshot will be displayed.

This window is quite important because it displays information on what is being imported into the project. We can select which files we want to import and which ones we don't. It also displays if the file is new, as in not already in the project, or old, meaning it's already in our **Assets** folder and is being updated. For now we need all the files from the package file, so go ahead and click on **Import**. The following screenshot shows Unity project after importing `ImageTarget`:

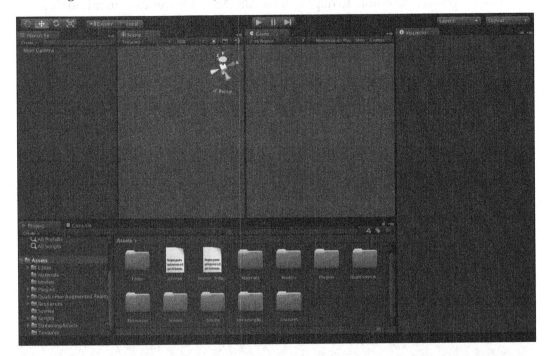

We can see that a lot of files have been imported into our **Assets** folder, including a **Qualcomm Augmented Reality** folder that is the Vuforia SDK. This is everything we need for a deployable project, but the scene hierarchy still only contains a **Main Camera** object and the **Game** panel is still quite blue. This is because we have loaded the assets but not the scene file yet.

Unity scene files

Scene files are essentially how Unity stores the scene hierarchy and composition. Scene files hold the world created in the editor with all its details. This is useful for loading different scene files at different times and creating multiple worlds, related or unrelated, in the same app. This is how Unity handles multiple game levels and areas.

Now to select the project's scene files that Qualcomm already created for us, we can go to the **Scenes** folder in the project files and double-click on the file named **Vuforia-4-ImageTargets**. The following screenshot shows the **Vuforia-4-ImageTargets** scene active:

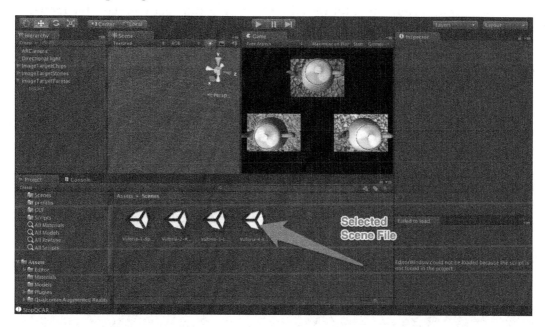

Now Unity project view looks much more lively. There are rendered 3D teapots already visible in the **Game** panel, and the **Hierarchy** panel displays the components of the scene. Chances are the **Scene** editor still looks empty as in the preceding figure; we will see now how to navigate to the **Scene** editor view to move around the world created.

The first thing we need to do is to focus on one of the objects we have in our scene to be our origin point. We can do that by selecting the first image target object from the **Hierarchy** panel, which is **ImageTargetChips**, then place the mouse pointer over the scene panel and press the keyboard button *F*. This will zoom over the object and have it as the origin point for the editor view. It is important to have the mouse pointer over the **Scene** panel, otherwise the zoom will not happen over the object. The following screenshot shows the selected object in focus:

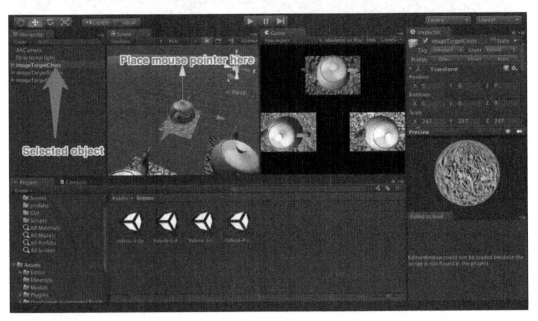

Now that the object is in focus, we can have the editor camera orbit around it to view the scene in game. We can do that by holding the *Alt* key and dragging over the scene to position the editor camera anywhere we like. We can also use the mouse wheel to zoom in and out of the object in focus.

As we can see, the scene is made up of three different teapots lying over a plane with an image over it. This is the AR scene that is in the sample project, which will display one of the teapots depending on the image target detected by ARCamera. The scaling and the transformation of the object will match that currently visible in the **Scene** editor in relation to the image target the teapot is on. This makes visualizing how the AR experience will play out very easy while building it.

Trackable files

In the project folder, we will find the trackable images used in this project. We will need to have them printed in order to test the AR experience. To reach them, navigate to **Assets | Editor | QCAR | ImageTargetEditor**. Inside there will be two folders with the three images used in the scene. To open them right-click on the image and select **Reveal in Finder** to open the file in Mac OS X finder. The following screenshot shows the target image location in the project:

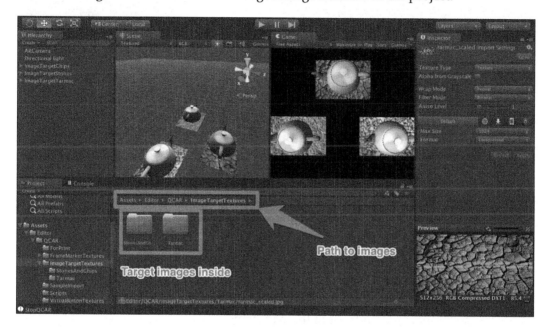

When printing the images, make sure that they fill the entire page to have the best result with the AR experience.

Vuforia has a handy feature that allows us to view the AR experience without the need to deploy first. This is achieved by having a web cam on the PC in use and Unity utilizes the information from the webcam to display how the experience will play out in the Game panel. This is indispensable for debugging AR projects without wasting time on deployment cycles.

To utilize this feature, simply click on the **Play Button** at the top of the Unity project window. The following screenshot shows live camera feed AR:

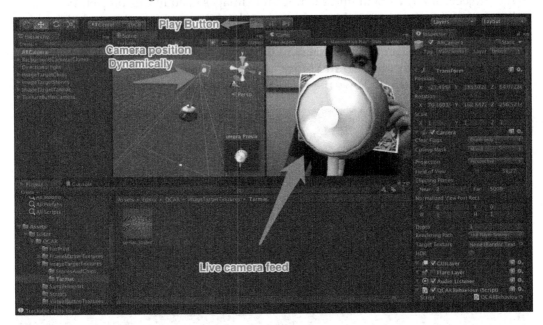

By having the target image in front of the camera, Vuforia will recognize the trackable and then position the ARCamera object relative to the target image and render the 3D content. If we click on the **ARCamera** component from the **Hierarchy** panel, we can see the ARCamera moving dynamically and relative to the target as we move the target image in front of the web cam.

The **ARCamera** is practically the window through which the user can view the world we create inside Unity. By moving the camera relative to the target image, we can effectively simulate that the teapot is part of the real world.

Try different targets to see how they respond differently by displaying the different teapots.

When we opened the **Scenes** folder, we found more than one scene. We only chose the **Main Scene**, but now it's time to understand what the other scenes are there for.

Open the **Scene** folder again from the **Assets** folder. The four scenes are named as follows

- `Vuforia-1-SplashScreen`
- `Vuforia-2-AboutScreen`
- `Vuforia-3-LoadingScene`
- `Vuforia-4-ImageTargets`

Apps are rarely made of one scene; usually they are a collection of scenes that play out in a certain succession. For this sample project, the app is made using four scenes. The first scene to appear to the user is the `SplashScreen` scene. The splash screen will only do what the name suggests; it will display a splash screen for the user for two seconds, then it will automatically load the next scene that is `AboutScreen`.

The `AboutScreen` scene will display an about screen about the app. It will have a button to dismiss the about screen and load the next scene, which is `LoadingScene`.

The loading scene does one simple task, which is to load the main scene, `ImageTarget`, in the background and display an animated spinner to indicate loading. This is always a good idea when loading a large scene. Without it, the app seems to freeze for a few seconds while loading the next scene; this might let the user think the app crashed or is unresponsive.

As we can see, the succession of the four scenes makes up the entire app experience. Feel free to open any of the scene files and click on the play button to see how they act individually. But if we do that, we will notice that the scenes do not load any scene behind it when the action is done; that is because we have not told Unity what scene files to load when the app starts. Right now if we deploy, we will only get a blue screen on the device because no scenes are loaded at all.

Build settings

To mark the scenes to be loaded with the app, we have to access the build settings window. To do this, navigate to **File | Build Settings**. The following screenshot shows the **Build Settings** window:

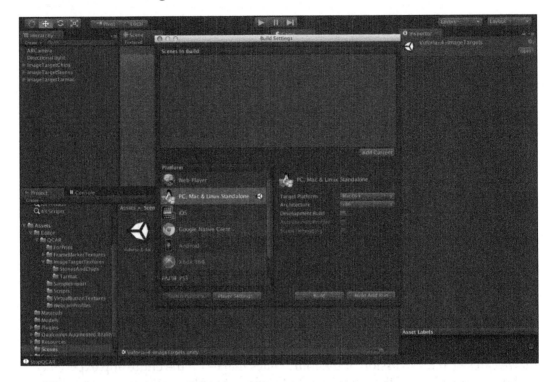

The **Build Settings** window is a very important one in Unity. From it, we can control what platform we are deploying for, what scenes to include in the deployment, the platform-specific settings, and even deploy on the platform from there.

The top box in the windows is where scenes are marked to be included in the app. Any scene the app will ever use must be added to this in the **Build Settings** window to work on the platform. We will add our scenes now, but first make sure that the box doesn't have any scenes in it. Scenes sometimes are added automatically if there were no scenes designated. Unity does that to avoid deploying the build with no scenes at all. To delete any scene, click on it and press backspace on the keyboard.

It is very important to know that the first scene in the window will be the first scene the app will open up to. This is very important to have right, or the flow of the app will be wrong. In our case, the SplashScreen scene is the first one. It loads the about screen after it. That mean we need to add the SplashScreen scene first to have the app open up to; the order of the scenes after it is not important since loading is done with the name of the scene in our project.

To add the scenes, simply drag the scene file from the scene folder to the window. Make sure you add the SplashScreen scene before adding any other scene. Add all the four scenes. The following screenshot shows **Build Settings**:

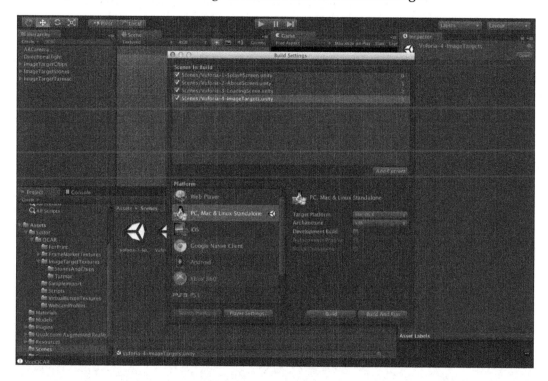

Notice the numbers next to the scenes in build; they are numerical representation of the scenes that can be used to load the scenes instead of their name. The number **0** represents the first scene that the app will load automatically.

Deploying for Android

We will be deploying to Android in this section; if for any reason you choose to not deploy on this platform, you can skip over to the next section that handles iOS.

Now that we have all the scenes added to the scenes in build, we move on to other settings in preparation for the deployment. Under the **Scenes in Build** window, there is an intriguing box with the name **Platform** that has a colorful collection of well-known platform. These are the platforms that Unity can deploy the project to. Some of them will be grayed out if we do not own the license to deploy to them from Unity. By default, the PC, Mac, and Linux standalone platform is selected. This obviously is not our target platform so we go ahead and change that.

Choose the **Android** platform, and then click on the **Switch Platform** button in the bottom-left corner. This will start the process of automatically converting all the assets to suit the new platform we just picked.

Once Unity has finished processing the assets, click on the **Player Settings...** button. In the **Inspector** panel, we will find something similar to the following screenshot:

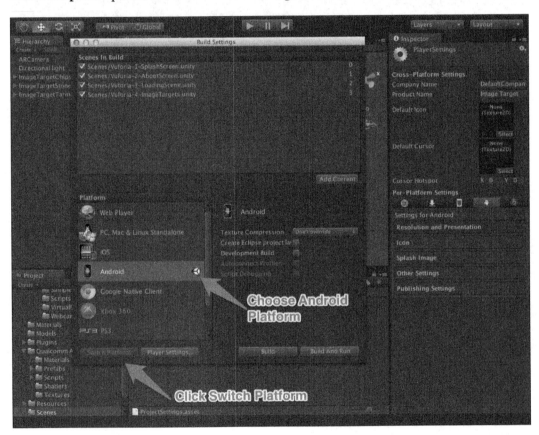

PlayerSettings reveals the target platform-specific settings, for example, the app name, splash screen, icons, and so on. It is important to customize the settings correctly for every platform we are deploying to, to achieve better results.

Change the app name in the **Product Name** field to `Image Target`. We will not customize the icons and splash images right now, though it is important to know that you can do so from here.

One of the most important settings that are particularly hidden in the panel is the app **Identification** field. We know that is important for an app to maintain its identity on the market and it is important to remember to set it correctly. To reach that setting, click on **Other Settings** as shown in the following figure:

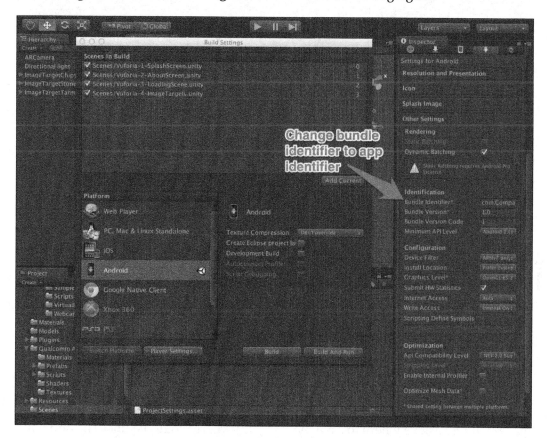

Change the **Bundle Identifier** to something suitable to the app. Notice that the other settings all handle very low-level settings regarding the platform, such as API level and what OpenGL to use. We can leave it at the default for now and it will work on most devices, but it pays off to know where to reach those settings in the future.

As we know, Android apps are deployed using keystores. Unity makes the process of creating one a little easier. To reach keystore settings, click on **Puslishing Settings** as shown in the following screenshot:

Now select **Create New Keystore**, and then enter any password in the two fields as shown in the preceding screenshot. This will tell Unity to create a new keystore for us and use it when deploying. It is important to note that Unity will not store our password for us; if we are to restart Unity, we will have to re-enter the password here or build will fail.

Now that everything is in place, we only need to click on **Build And Run** to deploy the app. It will ask us where to save the APK; anywhere would be fine. The app will be deployed to the Android device connected using USB to the machine, so we need to make sure it is properly connected.

If Unity failed to recognize the android device connected, make sure that the USB drivers for the specific device are correctly installed. They can be found on the manufacturer's website.

Deploying for iOS

Choose the iOS platform, and then click on the **Switch Platform** button at the bottom-left corner. You will notice Unity re-building and re-importing certain assets. This process is to match compression schemes and settings for the target platform. This is an automatic process that Unity handles very well on its own.

After Unity has finished importing all the assets again, its time to continue adjusting our settings to build the project on the device. At the bottom, there is a button named **Player Settings....** Click on this button to get something like the following screenshot:

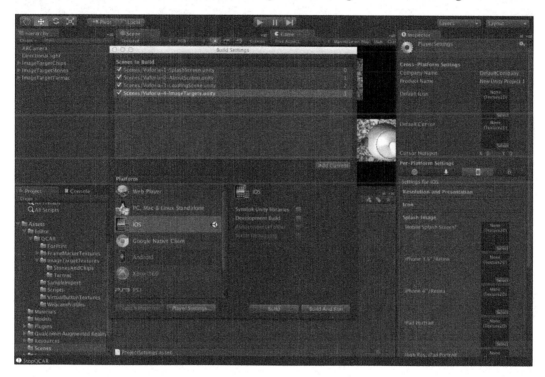

As with Android, **PlayerSettings** is where all the platform-specific settings you would expect are. It will include anything specific to iOS now that we have switched to the iOS platform.

First, let's change the app name. In **Product Name**, change it to Image Target. We will leave the default icon and splash screen for now. For now we adjust the **Resolution and Presentation** settings. Click on the **Resolution and Presentation** bar to expand the settings area.

In the **Default Orientation** section, choose from the drop-down box the **Auto Rotation** option. It will expand a list of checkboxes below it. Uncheck the first one which is **Use Animated Autorotation**. The following screenshot shows the **Resolution and Presentation** section:

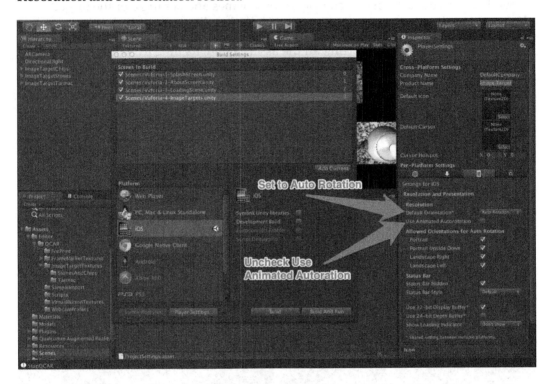

Resolution and Presentation settings handle the presentation of the app to the user. It has options such as supported device orientations and status bar visibility. We just enabled the auto rotation option for the app. We also disabled **Use Animated Autorotation** because it never looks OK for AR experiences. It is usually disorienting for the user.

Now what is left for us to do is set the bundle identifier for the app. Apple developer provisions are issued per app identifier, which follows this structure:

```
com.Company.ProductName
```

Depending on your Xcode managed provision company name, you need to input yours in Unity settings for deploying through Xcode works.

To reach the bundle identifier settings, click on the other bar at the very button of the **Inspector** area, and change the **Bundle Identifier** with a proper one that Xcode will accept. The following screenshot shows **Bundle Identifier** settings:

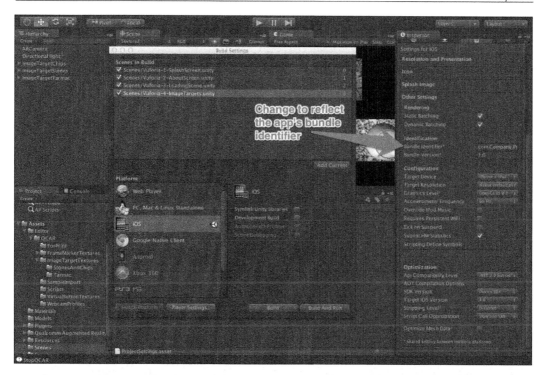

Now that we have gone through all the settings needed, it is time to deploy the app to the device. The process of deployment is very simple thanks to Unity's strong cross-platform capability. The process is mostly automatic and requires little to no interference from the developer.

First, connect the device to the PC. Now we click on the **Build and Run** button, in the **Build Settings** window, on the bottom-right. It will ask you where you want to have the build folder located; it is OK to just locate it inside the **Unity** project folder, but not inside the **Assets** folder. Give it any name you would like; it's a good convention though to name it like the **Unity** project folder name.

Unity will start an automated process of building the project for iOS. It will also open Xcode automatically. Try not to interfere with the process till the very end. The process of opening Xcode from Unity is done using a script, witch switches the focused window and executes certain steps on Xcode. So it is preferable to let Unity take control of your PC till it's done and not switch focus to any other window.

After Xcode has finished copying the app to the device, we should find a perfectly working AR app on our devices. The app will work exactly as we would expect it to, and displays how powerful the Unity and Vuforia combo is.

The following screenshot shows **About** screen of the Image Target app:

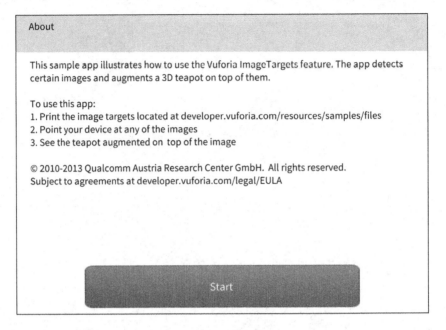

Note that when Unity is deploying to Xcode, it will automatically switch between open windows and execute a number of scripts on Xcode. This is why we need to let Unity do its routine and let it have control of the desktop till it starts building. If we forcefully prevent it from switching to Xcode automatically, it will interrupt automatic building. Note that it can be resumed manually after that.

Summary

In this chapter we have gone through the process of setting up our environment. We installed both Unity and Vuforia. We were introduced to Unity's GUI and started a new project. We imported Vuforia 's sample app and saw how to deploy it to our devices. While doing that, we were introduced to many Unity settings that relate to app deployment and also some basic features of Vuforia.

With this, we are familiar with the process of deployment and how the final products look. We have set up our environment to be able to build AR apps using Vuforia and Unity, and have seen how easy it is to deploy on the target device. We were introduced to simple settings for the Unity environment, and paved the way for a more in-depth look at how to build our own scenes and our own AR experiences.

In the next chapter, we will start to familiarize ourselves more with Vuforia and how to start a project from scratch.

3
Understanding Vuforia

In this chapter we will go over the components Vuforia provides with the SDK, and how to construct an AR scene. The addition of the SDK to a project will be covered, and how to include and activate the trackable data to be recognized in the app. We will create a very simple project from scratch similar to the example project provided by Vuforia to see how all the components fit together.

Creating a Unity project with Vuforia

From the previous chapter, we know how to create a project easily from Unity. Do not forget to exclude any spaces in the project name. This will create an empty project that we can build our AR app on.

By default, Unity projects are created preset to the PC and Mac stand-alone platform. We need to change that to iOS. The current platform is always visible on the window title bar on the top.

Downloading the example code

You can download the example code files for all Packt books you have purchased from your account at http://www.packtpub.com. If you purchased this book elsewhere, you can visit http://www.packtpub.com/support and register to have the files e-mailed directly to you.

The following screenshot shows platform switching.

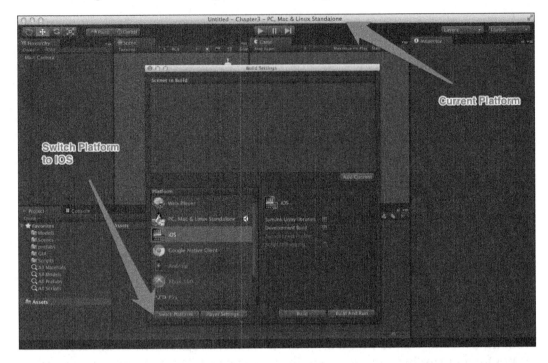

After switching the platform, it is time to add the Vuforia SDK to our project. To do that, click on the **Asset** menu in the menu bar, then inside **Import package ...**, click on **custom package**. This is exactly the same way we imported the sample project from Vuforia to our project.

Now find where Vuforia SDK was installed and choose the Vuforia Unity package to be imported into the project. The following screenshot shows the importing of a Vuforia package:

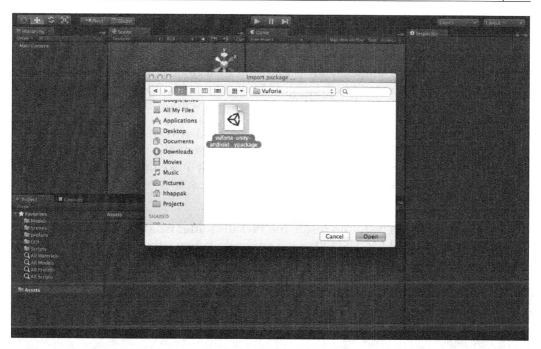

Now that the entire Vuforia library has been added to the project, we can start looking at the components that comes with it. All that makes a Vuforia project is within the **Qualcomm Augmented Reality** folder inside the project. This folder will contain all the scripts that control the behavior of the AR experience. Not only scripts, but some shaders and textures as well. They are mainly used for the video background rendering of the AR app.

Fortunately, we don't have to deal directly with most of those scripts, as Vuforia bundles the necessary components in Unity prefabs ready to be dropped into the scene.

Vuforia prefabs

A **prefab** is essentially a type of asset that is created in Unity to be a reusable game object stored in Project view. Prefabs can be inserted as many times as we want into the scene and with any object transformation applied to it. When added to the scene, they are basically an instance of the original prefab and linked to it. When a change is applied to the original prefab, all its instances will copy it, as they are essentially clones of it.

Prefabs are an indispensable tool for Unity. It makes the creation of standard scene components a much easier task. Imagine we are making a game with many enemy non-player characters. It will take a lot of time to manually construct every one of them, but if we create a single enemy prefab and then clone it multiple times, it will make constructing the scene much easier. Also if we want to edit the entire enemy NPCs, we only have to edit the prefab and the change will propagate.

Unity prefabs also make it easier to share components between projects if they are to be exported into Unity packages. This is essentially what Qualcomm did with Vuforia components. All the components that make the AR scene are stored as prefabs that are ready to be dropped into the scene; we only needs its parameters adjusted.

All Vuforia prefabs can be found inside the **Prefabs** folder inside the **Qualcomm Augmented Reality** folder. The following screenshot shows the **Qualcomm Augmented Reality Prefabs** folder:

Inside the **Prefabs** folder, we will find all the components explained before such as the **ImageTarget** prefab and the **FrameMarker** prefab. We will also find the **ARCamera** prefab, which is the common thing among any type of AR app.

By default, when Unity creates a new scene, it adds a camera to the scene such as the one in the **Hierarchy** panel. In our case, we will use Vuforia's special **ARCamera** prefab in our scene. So we need to first delete the **Main Camera** object from the **Hierarchy** panel.

Simply select the **Main Camera** from the scene **Hierarchy** and right click on it, then click on **Delete**. Now drag-and-drop the **ARCamera** prefab to the scene. Anywhere on the scene is fine. Now to focus on its position, select the **ARCamera** from the **Hierarchy** panel and hold the *F* keyboard key till the focus is on it. When holding the *F* key, make sure the mouse pointer is over the scene panel, or the focus will not work. The following screenshot shows **ARCamera** prefab added to the scene:

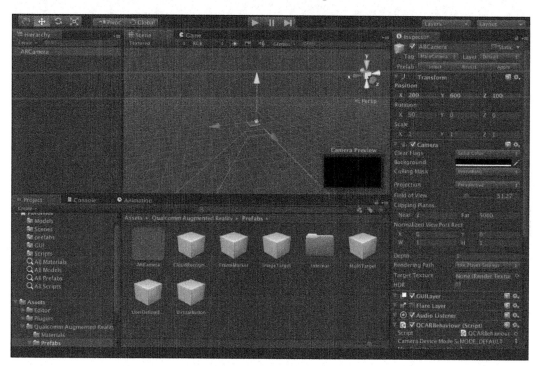

Adding the rest of the components is just as easy. Now that we have an **ARCamera** prefab added to the scene, we just need to add the **ImageTarget** prefab to the scene as well. Drag and drop the **ImageTarget** prefab anywhere on the scene.

This prefab is the platform that we will add the 3D content to. It will also hold the image target that the app will track to orient ARCamera the way we saw in the sample app. The following screenshot shows **ImageTarget** prefab added to the scene:

Depending on where the ImageTarget prefab was dropped in the scene, its position in the game world displayed in the transform section will differ. **Transform** is basically the position of the game object in the game world. Transform holds three different vectors for three different data about the position of the object. That data is as follows:

- **Position**: This is the position of the object in the three axes, x, y, and z
- **Rotation**: This is the rotation of the object in the three axes , x, y, and z
- **Scale**: This is the size scale of the object compared to its original size in the game world

Objects can be anywhere in the world, but it is recommended to keep the world's floor at *y=0*. By keeping the floor to 0, it simplifies a lot of other aspects of code when it comes to changing the transformation of object through scripts. So now change all the `ImageTarget`'s position to be (*x=0*, *y=0*, *z=0*). This will position the object in the origin of the world and simplifies the position aspect of subsequent game objects. The following screenshot shows the image target inspector:

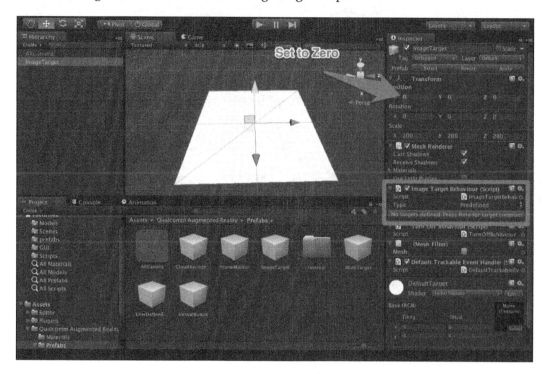

As it is noticeable from the inspector, there are a lot of settings for Image Target that might seem intimidating at first. One of those components is named **Image Target Behaviour (Script)**, which is highlighted in the image above; this is responsible for attaching the image target data to the image target object. Right now, it has no target defined in the app because we haven't added any yet, hence the white representation of the image target.

The first thing we need to do is to add the image target's data into the app. We do that by importing the dataset's Unity package that is available with the book content by the name `exampleDataset.unitypackage`. Import the package in the same way we imported all the other Unity packages. The following screenshot shows **exampleDataset.unityPackage**:

What this package essentially contains is the data of the target image that Vuforia's tracking algorithm can effectively look for from the camera's feed. It also carries a texture representation of the target image to be viewed inside Unity's editor while developing the app.

Now that the project contains the tracking data, a new selection will appear inside the `ImageTarget` prefab for the **Image Target Behaviour**. We will be able to select any of the images imported from the target package and the `ImageTarget` prefab will instantly adopt it.

First we need to select the dataset that contains the images. From the dropdown menu, we can select the only dataset available, named **exampleDataset**. From the dropdown menu below, we can choose the specific target image. Choose the target image stones. Notice immediately the **ImageTarget** representation in the game world carries now the target image. The following screenshot shows the dataset selection:

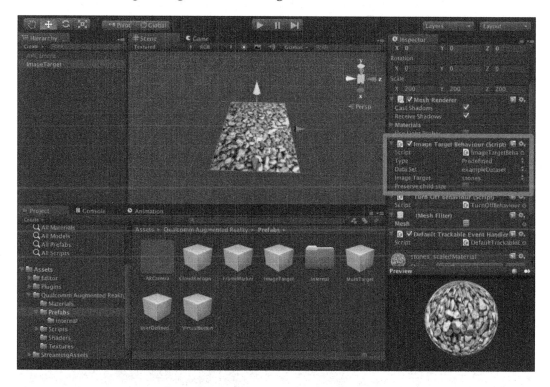

Datasets are essentially a collection of image targets that Vuforia will track simultaneously for any of the images inside it. Inside the dataset that we imported, we have images images from the Vuforia sample project. The app will track all three images at any given time till it finds any of the images to render the 3D material on top of it.

The app can have multiple datasets with as many as 100 images in each one of them. That is a substantial number of images that Vuforia can track. We also have the ability to activate and deactivate any of the datasets from the editor or from script.

When we added the dataset to the `ImageTarget`, it represented the image target in the world right away, but that doesn't necessarily mean that `ARCamera` will be tracking that dataset. For that, we need to first activate the dataset and tell the `ARCamera` to start tracking that dataset.

Click on the **ARCamera** object from the **Hierarchy** panel. In the inspector, we can find the **Script** component **Data Set Load Behaviour (Script)**. Inside the component, there will be one checkbox with the label **Load Data Set exampleDataset**. If we click on the checkbox, another one will appear with the label **Activate**. Click on that as well. Now the dataset is loaded and activated. The following screenshot shows the activated dataset in **ARCamera**.

There is a particular reason why we need to both load and activate the datasets as separate options. The datasets will be loaded but not necessarily tracked at the start of the scene if added to the `ARCamera` component. From script, we can then enable and disable tracking for any of them without the need for loading overhead. The process is very fast that way.

Now we know that Vuforia both knows what trackables to track and is actively tracking them. We added the `ImageTarget` prefab and set it to the **Stones** image target. If we are to press play and present the camera with the stones image target, nothing will happen beyond a console log declaring it has detected the image target. We might even notice the `ARCamera` frantically moving around the game world in relation to the image target in the editor. That is simply because we do not have any 3D content attached to the target image just yet.

Importing and attaching 3D objects

Unity is capable of importing 3D models from many well-established formats. Models can be created from any of the 3D modeling applications such as 3D max, Maya, and Blender. As long as the model is exported in a Unity-supported format, it is easily imported into the project.

Formats supported by Unity are as follows:

- Maya (`.mb` and `.ma`)
- 3D Studio Max (`.max`)
- Cheetah 3D (`.jas`)
- Cinema 4D (`.c4d`)
- Blender (`.blend`)
- Modo (`.lxo`)
- Autodesk (`.fbx`)
- COLLADA
- Carrara
- Lightwave
- XSI 5.x
- SketchUp Pro
- Wings 3D
- 3D studio (`.3ds`, does not work on Mac OSX)
- Wavefront (`.obj`)
- Drawing Interchange Files (`.dxf`)

The list is quite extensive. It is quite safe to assume that Unity will support most known 3D model formats. Notice though that Unity uses the 3D modeling application to convert the model format to FBX, which then can be imported by Unity. This process is mostly automatic and produces smooth results and streamlines the workflow considerably.

Now it's time to add our own 3D model to the project. Firstly, we need to create a folder for models in our project. We will use it to include all models in our project. In the **Assets** root folder, create a folder and name it Models.

Importing assets is easily done from the **Assets** menu at the top. Click on **Import New Asset** from the menu, and point at the chapter's assets folder and choose frog.fbx file. Unity will start importing the asset right away. The following screenshot shows Unity imported **Frog** asset:

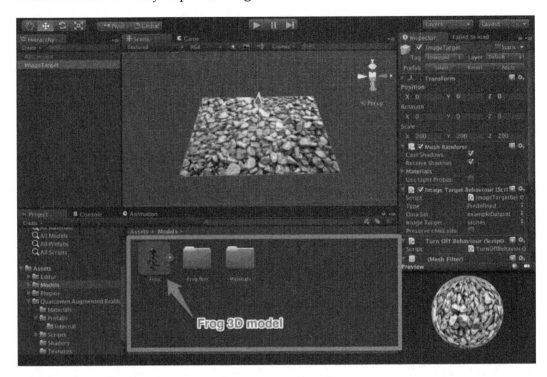

Now we have the 3D model in our project, it is that easy to add models to Unity projects. That is good news because for a game engine, adding models is one of the top chores done in projects. Are you wondering why the 3D model is a frog? It is because it's generally good for developers to have a sense of humor; it helps.

When importing the 3D model, it created two folders and one file for us. The folders contain materials for the 3D model and settings for the FBX import. The file is actually a Unity prefab of the model with the materials attached ready to be dropped to the scene. Unity creates the prefab automatically for us.

Now we can drag the **Frog** prefab and drop it in our scene. The frog 3D model will appear in our game world. The following screenshot shows the frog model added to the scene:

Just as when we added the ImageTarget prefab, the frog's position in the scene is almost certainly not right. We need to position it on top of the ImageTarget and for it to face the right way, but first we need to approximate its position in relation to the ImageTarget better. Remember when we added the ImageTarget; we positioned it at the game world's origin at (0,0,0) position. We will do the same for the frog as a first step.

Select the frog from the **Hierarchy**, and from the inspector panel in **Transform** position, set x, y and z to zero. The following screenshot shows the frog position at the origin point:

The first thing to notice wrong with the frog is that it is sunk in the ImageTarget. The other problem is that it is too small for the ImageTarget.

First we will try to position the frog above the ImageTarget. At the top left of Unity, make sure that you have the directional cross button selected. This allows us to change the position of the selected object. Notice the green, blue, and red axes coming out of the frog. They are the relative position of the object in the game world. Green is for the y axis, red for the x axis, and blue for the z axis. We will want to move the object in the y axis to get it above the ImageTarget. To do that, simply drag the green axis and move the mouse up; the object will move up with it.

Position the frog anywhere above the `ImageTarget`. It doesn't have to be perfect for now. The following screenshot shows the frog positioned higher in the y axis:

Now for the second problem, its size; we will need to scale it up considerably to fit the `ImageTarget`.

While the frog is selected from the scene, click on the **Scale** button from the top left menu. It is the last icon on the right of a square with arrows coming out of it.

The scaling button allows us to scale the object in the scene on any axis or all axes. Since we need the object to scale in every direction equally to avoid the frog being stretched in one direction more than the other, we need to click on the square at the origin of the three axes now represented on the object, and then drag the mouse over it. The following screenshot shows the scaled up the frog object:

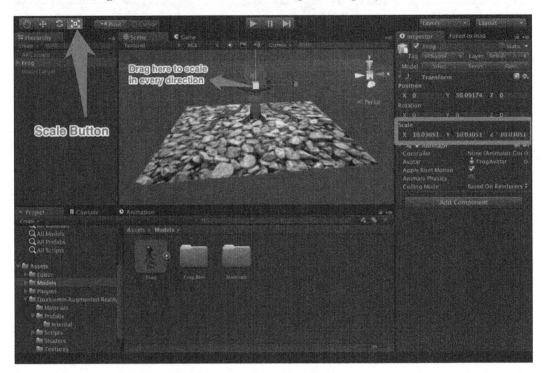

Scaling up to 10 in the inspector should be sufficient, but since there are no constraints, we can make it as big or as small as we want it to be.

Now, we need to make the frog face the right way, opposite to where it's facing right now. To do that we need to activate the Rotation button in the top left menu.

Once the Rotation button is activated, the axes over the object will look quite different. For a start they are spherical in nature, and there are more than just the (x, y, and z) axes.

Rotation functions in a similar manner, despite the different look to the other transformation tools. By dragging on the (x, y, and z) axes, we can rotate the object around any of the three axes. The remaining white axes are diagonal rotations for easy access.

Drag the green y axis to rotate the object to face the right way. Notice the rotation data in the inspector changing around the y axis. We need it to be around `180` or `-180` degrees. Note that we can just input that number in the rotation section of the inspector to reach the same result. The following screenshot shows the rotated frog object:

Now that the frog is rotated to face the right way in relation to the trackable, we only need to position it higher up to be right on top of the trackable. We can achieve that in the same way we positioned the frog before. Only this time with more care and we must rotate the editor camera several times to make sure the frog is positioned from all angles correctly. The following screenshot shows correctly the positioned frog:

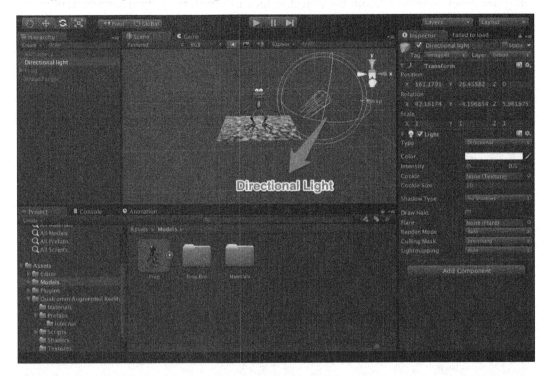

Now the frog is positioned perfectly fine on top of the image target, all is good. You would notice, though, that the frog seems to have dull colors. That is mainly due to the lack of any light sources in the scene; this is what we are going to add next.

From the top menu, choose **GameObject**. From the menu click on **Directional Light** from the **Create Other** menu. This adds an object called Directional Light to your scene. The following screenshot shows Directional Light added to scene:

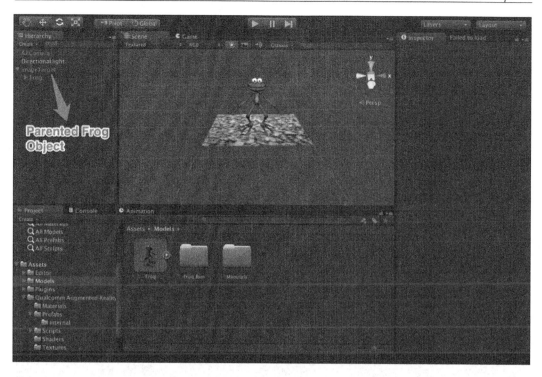

Directional Light is a type of scene light that is quite easy to add and cheap on device resources. It essentially acts like a sun, lighting up any object in the direction you point it at. All we need to do is adjust the object's rotation. Its position in the game world doesn't mean much, because its light is only based on its direction, not its position.

Now the frog is where we want it to be, and looking good. We might be tempted to press the **Play Button** now and test the AR experience. If we do that and present the camera with the trackable, the frog will appear correctly. But once the trackable is lost to the camera, we will find that the frog remains on the screen regardless. This happens because we did not parent the frog with the image target.

Parenting in Unity objects

There is a good reason Unity's **Hierarchy** panel is named that way. That is because it represents the object's hierarchy in the scene. If we are to click on the arrow next to the frog object in the **Hierarchy** panel, it will reveal a number of objects below it. These objects are essentially children of the object frog.

The parent object frog contains many children under it in **Hierarchy** that essentially means that the children's transformation will follow that of the parent. When we moved the frog object around, we didn't have to individually move the children as we did so; they automatically moved with the parent object. That is fortunate because it would have consumed a lot of time to do that.

Parenting in Unity happens for a number of reasons. Whether it's script access, transformation, or simple grouping, Unity parenting is a very important feature.

For image targets to work correctly, we must parent them over any 3D content they will display. This is a must for Vuforia to be able to control when and how the 3D content is shown to match that of the image target.

To parent it, we simply need to drag the frog object and drop it over the `ImageTarget` object in the **Hierarchy** panel. The following screenshot shows the parented frog object:

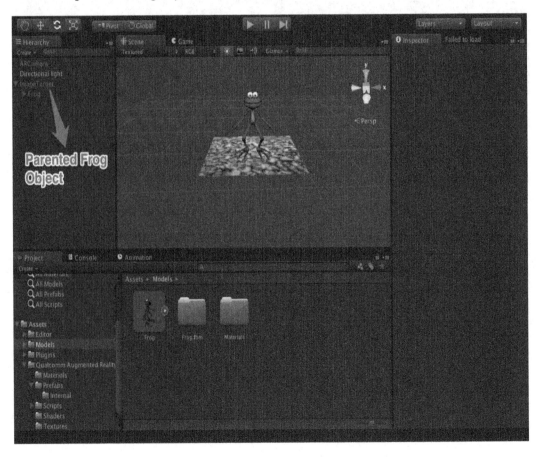

With that our AR project should be functional and displays the frog correctly once we click on the **Play Button** to test it. We can deploy it on the device if we follow the settings explained in the previous chapter.

Through this chapter, we have learned how to build a Vuforia project from scratch in Unity, how to import and present our 3D objects, and how to add and set up Vuforia components to correctly display it.

Summary

In this chapter, we started our new Unity project that we added Vuforia SDK to. We were introduced to the meaning of the term prefab and then explored the different prefabs that are packaged inside Vuforia SDK. We saw how to build up an AR scene using Vuforia prefabs, especially the ARCamera prefab and ImageTarget prefab. We then understood the method in which we add targets to the project and how to activate those datasets in our project. We also saw how easy it is to add a 3D model to a Unity project and position it in our scene however we like and add appropriate lightening.

Next chapter, we will see how to create our own target datasets in the target manager, and understand how to obtain the best targeting results from the images we choose.

4
Trackables and Tracking

Trackables are an integral part of an AR experience. It is the foundation on which the whole world we are building literally rests. We can have the best AR content in the world, but if the trackable is not suitable, the experience will degrade considerably. In this chapter we will try to understand the details of how to create and use suitable trackables. We will also explore how to modify a trackable to increase its trackability in the app.

What are trackables for image targets?

Trackables are a collection of features that the AR app can track. This can be anything from the traditional QR code, where a collection of black and white binary code determines the object detected, to the image targets we experienced in the previous chapter where the trackable is just an image.

For image targets, only the natural features of the image itself is used as a way of detecting the image in the real, and its perspective to calculate where the AR camera should be. Natural features are analyzed, stored in a database, and then used to compare with the camera input feed. This naturally makes how effectively the image can be tracked, based on its features.

Creating image targets

The process is made simple using Vuforia's **Target Manager**. The target manager is an online tool provided by Qualcomm that automatically analyzes and creates image target databases to be deployed in apps. It can also manage multiple datasets with multiple targets.

To reach this target manager, simply go to the following URL:
`https://developer.vuforia.com/target-manager`.

The following screenshot shows **Target Manager**:

You should be greeted with a view similar to the one above. This is the target manager—the tool that we will use to create all of our targets and maintain them. The target manager can be used for both local target datasets and cloud-based ones. In this book, we will focus on **Device Databases**.

To start, let's create a database that we will use to see how the process of creating targets works. Click on the **Create Database** button and name the database Chapter 4. The following image shows a created dataset in **Target Manager**:

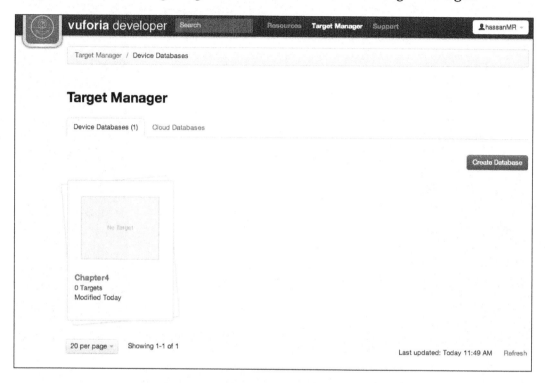

Now we have a dataset. Currently our dataset is empty, but we can add multiple image targets to a dataset for the AR app to track all of them. We can even create multiple datasets in this view, each with its own set of targets.

Now what we need to do is to create our first image target. First, we will use the stones image from Vuforia's sample project we did earlier. It will give us an idea of how the image targets for the sample project were created.

Click on the database to open it. We will find an add a target button on the right; click on it. The following image shows target creation:

The parameters for creating a target are very simple. For the name, we will pick Stones, like it was in the sample app. For target type, we will leave it at Single Image. The other two types are used for MultiTarget prefab in Vuforia for detecting 3D objects in the world.

The last parameter, Target Dimension, is an important parameter. This number is the representation of the image target in the scene. It governs how objects that appear on top of it are scaled, and how much space it occupies of the virtual space in the scene. That said, it is a value easily ignorable in Unity 3D environment. This is due to the scaling property that is easily editable in Unity. This value is very important in OpenGL environment however. For now, we can leave it at 5 units. This is a 5 units distance in the Unity 3D scene.

Click on the **Add** button, and let the image be uploaded. The target will have processing tag on it; processing takes a few minutes to happen. Give it some time, and then click on the target to see its details window. The following image shows Stones target details window:

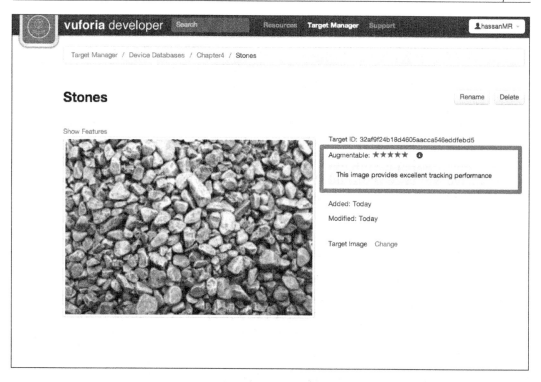

This is the details window of the target we just added to the database. To the right, we will find all the details about the target. It starts with a unique ID of the target across all databases, cloud-based and local. This is useful for global identification of the target.

Below the **Target ID**, we will find the augmentable score. This is the most important feature of the target. It demonstrates how well the target can be tracked in the app. This target has 5 stars out of 5; this is because the features in image are great for tracking.

Trackable score

Several factors affect the trackable score, but first we need to understand how the score affects the trackability for the image.

The augmentable score is based on 5 stars. It represents augmentability as follows:

- **Between 4 to 5 stars**: The trackable is very suitable for AR apps. It can handle part of the image to be occluded, and still the app will be able to track it. It can also be tracked in low light and other environment noise.

- **Between 2 to 3 stars**: The trackable is augmentable. It will work fine under ideal conditions. It may not be very good with part of the images occluded. This is the least score to aim for that will not affect the user's experience.

- **1 star**: This is the bare minimum score for trackability. It means that the image will be recognizable by the app, but the experience will be affected. Avoid attaining this score at all costs.

- **0 stars**: The image is not suitable for trackability at all; there are not enough recognizable features in the image for the app to recognize. This image will not be recognized at all by the app.

In situations where the content of the trackable is restricted, and we know that the usage conditions will be idle in good lighting with no occlusion, we can aim for 2 to 3 stars. Otherwise, it is preferable to get 4 to 5 stars for optimal usage by the user. Anything below 2 stars should be avoided completely.

What decides trackable score?

Trackables are the foundation of the AR experience using Vuforia. It is paramount to understand and create a suitable trackable for the experience to be robust and useful. The score attributed to the trackable in the target manager is our indication of how robust the target image is going to perform, but what decides that score?

The best way of understanding this, is by understanding how Vuforia tracks the images. The idea is simple; it looks for position of contrasting edges in clusters all around the image. Those edges are tracked, and based on the map of positions that are stored in the dataset, Vuforia can tell the relative position of the trackable in the real world, and accordingly render the 3D content on top of it. This particularly means that tracking the image is not a function of its color or what really is in it, as much as how many contrasting edges are there in the image, and how well they are distributed on the image.

To better understand this, we can look on the current edges that are recognizable in the image we have just uploaded. To do that, simply click on the **Show Features** link on the top left of the webpage. The following image shows features in image target stones:

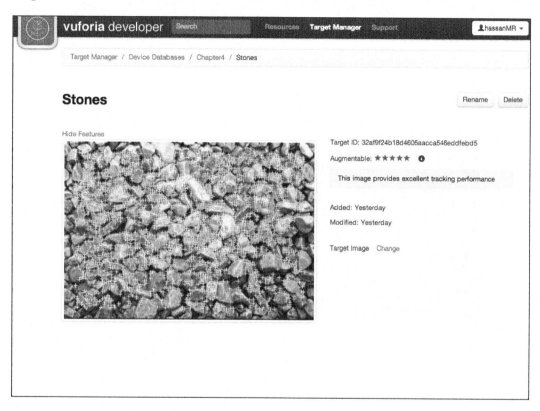

Once the **Show Features** link has been clicked, the image target manager layers over the target image an overlay of where it detects a recognizable edge that it can track in a Vuforia image target. Notice that it is only tracking the dark edges between the Stones and nothing else in the image. It is even tracking only the high contrast edges between the Stones, while ignoring some of the lighter ones.

Also notice that the number of edges found in the image is large, and evenly distributed all around the image. This is a great factor in what made this image suitable for tracking.

To contrast this image's result, lets try an image that will yield a 1-star score when tried on the target manager. The following image shows landscape image added to target image:

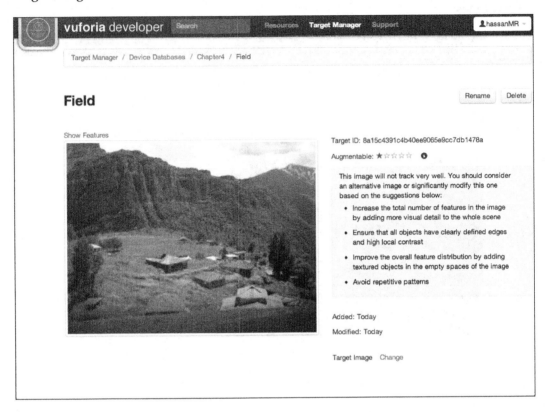

Before adding this image, intuitively, we might think that this image is suitable for tracking. It certainly has a lot of details of a wide-angle landscape. But this image yielded a shocking 1-star result when added to the **Target Manager**.

The main reason for the low score for this image is the fact that the entire image is a shade of green. This greatly diminishes contrasting edges in the image.

If we are to click on the **Show Features** link on the top, we will be able to see what the target manager detected from the image. The following image shows features in the mountain landscape image:

Immediately, we notice the considerably lower number of features detected in the image compared to the stones one. It only detected the edges created by the shadows of the objects in the image, which is clearly not enough to award it any score above 1 star.

Features definition

To help us get a higher score, we must understand what are the features that the target manager is looking for. We do know now that the main thing that the target manager is looking for in an image is edges, but what kind of edges specifically? To understand that, we need the definition of features.

A feature is a sharp and spiked detail in the image, like the corner of an edge. Features must be very contrasting to be found and it has to be distributed evenly across the image and in a random manner. The following image shows shapes and features recognized in them:

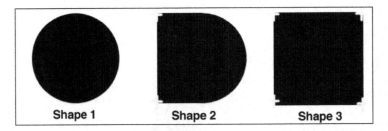

In the shapes illustrated above, we can see the yellow crosses representation of the features recognizable in the shape. The representation is as follows:

- **Shape 1**: It is a perfect circle without any corners at all, and as such, no features are recognizable in it.

- **Shape 2**: It has an edge to the left with two recognizable corners. That yields two features recognizable in the shape.

- **Shape 3**: It is a square with four edges and four corners. This yields four recognizable features in the shape.

This means that any curved object yields little to none features at all. Primarily, humans and animals make very poor trackables due to their curved nature.

Enhancing score by enhancing contrast

One of the easiest ways of enhancing an image's score is by simply enhancing the image's contrast. Feature detection looks for sharp edges like above; it is very hard to do so when the image's contrast is low. Like the landscape image we used before, the main reason the image resulted in a low score was because of the low contrast in the image. Then what happens when we increase the image's contrast and light levels in a photo editing application like Photoshop or Gimp? The following image shows the figure with enhanced contrast in landscape image:

The score makes a giant leap from 1-star score to 4-star score. As you can see, if you compare the image used now to the one we used earlier, the image's contrast is greatly enhanced, and the target manager easily detects such shadows and edges now. Lets look at the features detected by the target manager. The following image shows features in the high contrast image:

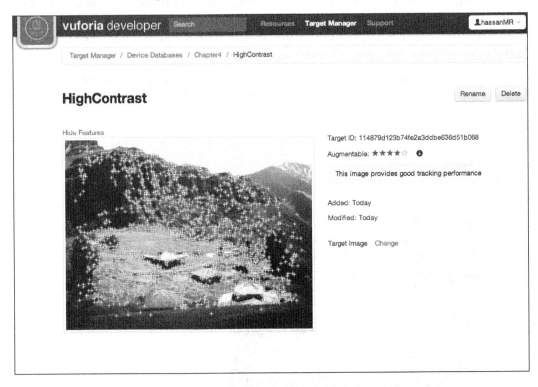

The features detected in the image are way more than what the target manager found in the previous image. Mostly, the features are located around the mountain and tree shadows. Notice how the green field is still yielding little features, but the features from the mountain and trees are enough to yield a high score of 4 stars.

It is highly recommend to enhance the contrast in all targets used for AR apps. It is greatly beneficial for the experience to have the best trackable possible.

Feature distribution on image targets

Having recognizable features on the image is important, but how they are distributed is also very important. We can have all the features recognized on only one part of the image and nothing on another. This kind of imbalance lowers the score greatly, because it hinders the detection of the relative position of the image in the world for the AR app. For example, examine the image target below.
The following image shows the lake target:

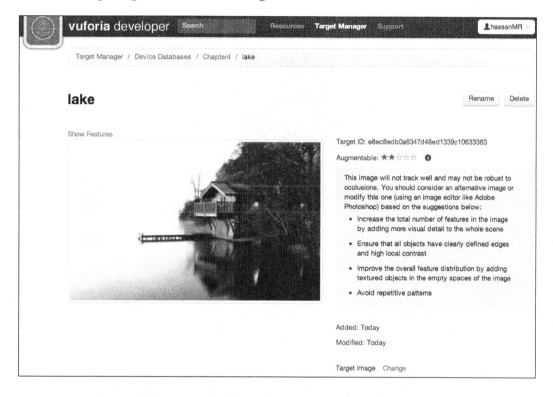

This is a lake image target that was added to the image target manager. It has a fair bit of details, but the left side of the image is mostly empty but for the lake. This image yielded 2 stars, and that is after enhancing the image's contrast.

To understand the reason for the low score, lets look at the features detected. The following image shows features in the lake house target:

As expected, all the features detected are on the right side of the image, leaving the left side completely empty. This is very bad for occlusion management and relative position detection by the AR app. It will track, but it will be a very poor target.

How to enhance distribution of features

Enhancing distribution of features can be done by the obvious method, which is adding objects to the empty space of the image. If we are to add textured objects to the empty side of the image above, it will naturally enhance its score after the new object yields new detectable features. But changing the target's composition might not always be a viable option in practice if there is a restriction on what the target can be. For example, if the target is part of a magazine or a brochure, and we do not have control on what we can add to the image. However, we will always have control on what we can subtract from the target.

If we manage to subtract the empty space from the image target and take a subset of the target that is rich in details and well-distributed features, we can circumvent the problem. The interesting part is that the AR app will trigger on the large image just fine, even if we only give data of the subset. For example, examine this subset target of the lake target we added earlier. The following figure shows a subset of the lake image target:

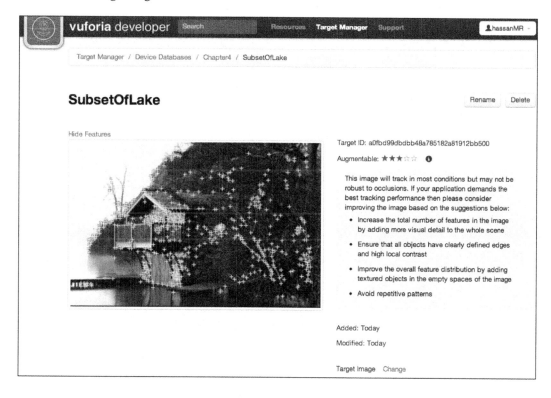

As we can see, the above image is only a subset of the lake image, with just the lake house visible in it. Immediately, more features are recognizable now that target manager can focus on a smaller area. It also enhanced the feature distribution on the image. This enhanced the score to 3 stars for this trackable.

The AR app will trigger to this image, regardless if it's in this subset form, or if it was subjected to the original image before cropping the lake house from it. This is a very useful feature to keep in mind when trying to achieve a higher score for a target.

The position of the AR content will need to be adjusted according to appear relative the original lake image and not the subset. This can be achieved easily with an offset to the position applied to the AR content in Unity.

Patterns in image targets

We now understand the need for a good distribution of features on the image, but there is one thing to keep in mind: having repeated patterns on the image is only counted once, meaning if we have a repeated pattern all across the image target, the score will be very bad. Examine the following image target. The following figure shows a snowflake pattern image target:

The above image when used yields a staggering 0 star. This image is mainly a repeated pattern of a snowflake. If we examine the features detected, we will see something like the following image. The following figure shows features in snowflake pattern:

As we can see, there are enough features detected in the image to effectively be augmentable, but yet the target manager gives it a 0 star. It will not be detectable at all from the app's perspective.

To understand why that happens, we need to ask ourselves the following question: if we take a subset of the image at the center, would it be distinguishable from the larger image? The answer is no, the pattern repeats itself symmetrically around the image. The app will not be able to find the relative position of the target in the real world if it compares the features detected with that in the dataset.

Exporting datasets to Unity

Now that we know how to select and create our trackables, exporting them to Unity is a much easier task. The following figure shows highlighted targets to be exported:

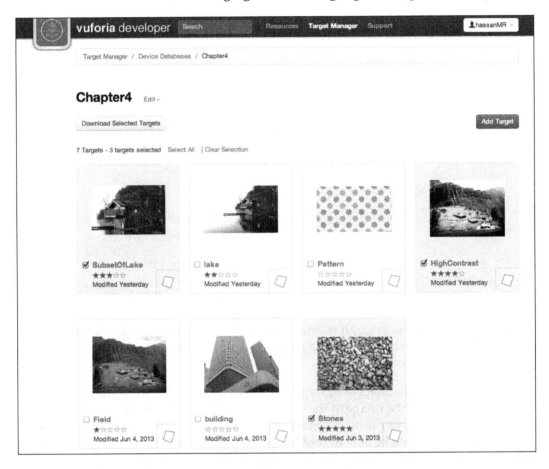

From the dataset's view, we can select what targets we want to export. Simply select any number of targets for deployment. Once the targets are selected, we can click on **Download Selected Targets** on the top left. The following image shows **Download Selected Targets**:

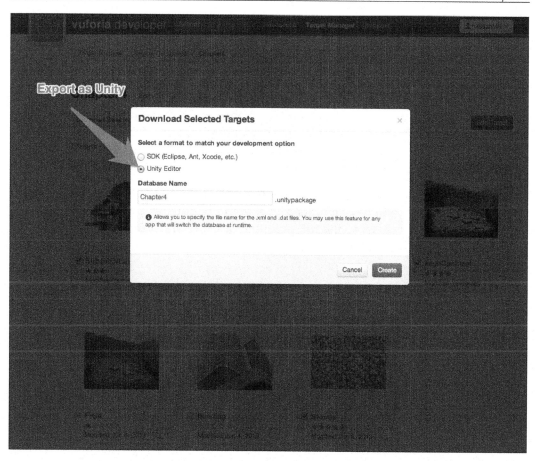

From the list of development option, select **Unity Editor** as the option. It is recommended to leave the database name the same name in the target manager. This makes it easier to update the dataset later. This will download a Unity package file that we can import easily into a project like we did in the sample project.

As we have seen, the create of a dataset in the target manager is quite easy, and makes creating a project more fluid.

Summary

In this chapter, we understood the process of creating our own trackables and datasets using the target manager from Qualcomm. We also explored how to design and use a trackable that will yield the best trackability in our apps. We have seen what makes a trackable bad, such as patterns and feature distribution, and what makes it good, such as contrast, and edges. We learned a couple of tricks to enhance the trackability score of our trackable, such as taking a subset of the original image or by increasing the contrast in Photoshop or apps like it. With this knowledge, we easily optimize the most important foundation of AR, which is our trackable.

In the next chapter, we will create a project from the scratch that will be an AR game. Techniques and code will be of a higher level than previously explored in the book so far, and will get us closer to the full potential of Unity and Vuforia.

5
Advanced Augmented Reality

There are a lot of possibilities for delivering augmented reality experiences. In this chapter, we will discuss a lot of the advanced features that are available when using Vuforia with Unity. We will do that while developing a small arcade augmented reality game. The game is a classic arcade game, with an augmented reality twist that will make it feel fresh. We will be making an augmented reality whack a mole game.

Augmented reality games

A lot of developers misunderstand the value of augmented reality games. Many view AR games as unprofitable and marginalized due to the fact that most, if not all, AR games cannot go viral and tend to not sell. This might be true due to the fact that AR games tend to require motion, a trackable, or both, like in the game we will now make. Those requirements make the game not playable at any time by the user, but what a lot of people tend to overlook is that it is ok for AR games not to go viral.

AR games, while not going to spawn the next Angry Birds, can deliver a unique experience for a specific purpose. For example, AR games can be used quite effectively for promotion games. The game can trigger on a promotion flyer or a page in the magazine and then a competitive game spawns up with a chance to win a real prize, for example. This insures that the user received a positive experience in the form of a fresh AR game, and at the same time, we are sure the user viewed the promotion and joined a competition. AR games can also be used in exhibitions or stores for many uses: promotional or pure entertainment.

Unity as a game engine

Surely Unity makes making AR apps easier and deployable to multiple platforms, but that is not where its true power comes from. Unity is first and foremost a very powerful modern game engine. It is used to power some of the industry's known games, both on mobile and PC. Not utilizing that kind of power to deliver very fresh AR experiences is inexcusable, because it is quite easy to understand how the engine works.

In this chapter, we will go over some of the elements in Unity that allow the making of simple games. We will go over how to add audio effects to the game, how to animate objects, how to set the world's physics, how to control particle effects, and how to factor in user interactions. Hopefully that will be enough to display how effective it is to build an AR game in Unity.

Setting up the environment

Now, we can start a new Unity project for the Whack-A-Mole game that we are creating. Like we did previously in the book, we set up Unity's environment for the AR app. The following are the steps again:

1. Change the value of **Platform** to **IOS** from the **Build Settings** under the **File** menu.

2. Import Vuforia Unity package by navigating to **Import Package | Assets**.

3. Import the `exampleDataset.unitypackage` file that we used previously in *Chapter 3, Understanding Vuforia*, that contains the dataset for trackables. They are available in this chapter's assets too.

4. Add **ARCamera** and **ImageTarget** prefabs from the **Qualcomm Augmented reality** prefab folder.

5. Set the **ImageTarget** to use the dataset we have imported, and set it to use **Chips** target from the **Inspector**.

6. Set **ARCamera** to load our dataset and activate it as well.

7. Save the scene to the **Assets** folder, and name it `Level`.

The following screenshot shows created the project for our Whack-A-Mole game:

We should end up with similar settings for the environment, as shown in the preceding screenshot. Now it is ready for us to start adding the elements that will make up our game.

The Whack-A-Mole game

In this section, we will go over the design of the game we are making. It is a simple Whack-A-Mole game with a twist. Over our target, we want to render a ground filled with mole holes, where the moles will pop up and down randomly from them. The user will be able to shoot balls at the moles from the device to the target; if a ball hits a mole, we will make the mole disappear with a sound effect and spawn a particle effect.

There will be no score system or a way to actually clear the level. We will just have this game as a demonstration of how games are made for AR in a simple way. All assets used in this game are available in the Assets folder in the code bundle of this chapter.

Creating the ground for moles

The first thing we need to do is to create the ground level from which moles will pop up. We need to create a plane that will be layered right on top of the trackable with a ground texture attached to it.

1. Let's create a plane from the **GameObject** menu. Choose **Create other** and click **Plane**. This will create a plane in the scene. Make sure the plane we created has the same position as the trackable; both should be at the global origin, which is at (0, 0, 0).

2. Now, resize the plane like we have done before by clicking on the **Resize** button at the top-left toolbar. Resize the plane so that its width exactly covers the trackable. The height of the plane most likely will be bigger than the trackable, but that is all right as long as the trackable is completely covered in the scene. The following screenshot shows the Z-Buffer distortion:

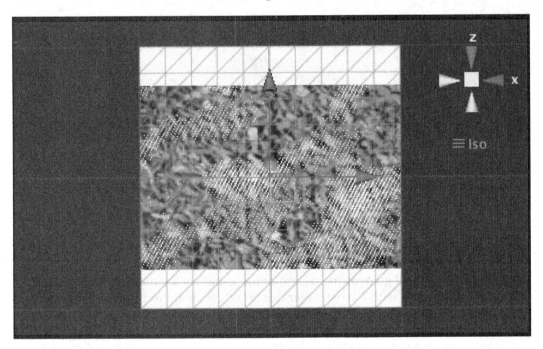

We might have noticed that the distortion that is happening between the trackable and the plane we just added. This is because both the trackable and the plane have the exact same position in the y axis. The engine doesn't know which one to render on top of the other, and something called **Z-Buffer conflict** happens, where the engine keeps on alternating between the components to be rendered on the top. The solution is to simply adjust the plane's y axis position to be slightly above that of the trackable.

1. Name the plane `Ground`, and attach it to the trackable by dragging-and-dropping it from the **Hierarchy** list to **ImageTarget**.

2. Now that the ground plane is in place, the first thing we will get the urge to do is to lose that plain white texture that is there by default on the plane. We would want it to look like an actual ground, so we will create a material for it. Materials for Unity are components that carry the information of what is the texture of the object and what shader is used to render it. It is very important and used extensively for almost every object in any scene.

3. First, create two folders in the **Assets** folder of our project from Unity. Name one `Textures`; this is where we will keep the texture images of our materials, and the other `Materials`; this is where we are going to create our materials.

4. Now drag-and-drop the file named **Ground.jpg** into the **Textures** folder we just created. We could also add the asset through the **Assets** menu, like we saw before. This just added the texture image for the ground to our project.

5. Now, let's create the material; inside the **Materials** folder we just created, from the **Assets** menu, choose **Material**. This creates a new material that we will name as `Ground`. Now attach the **Ground** material we created to the ground plane. Do this by simply dragging the material and dropping it on **Ground** plane in the **Hierarchy** panel.

Notice that the plane stays white as it was before; this is because we haven't attached the texture yet to the material. To do that, access the material we just added to the **Ground** plane by selecting the **Ground** plane and from the **Inspector**; here we will find the **Material** we assigned. There is a small **Texture** property under **Material**, drag-and-drop the texture we added earlier to this box. The following screenshot shows the **Ground** material attached:

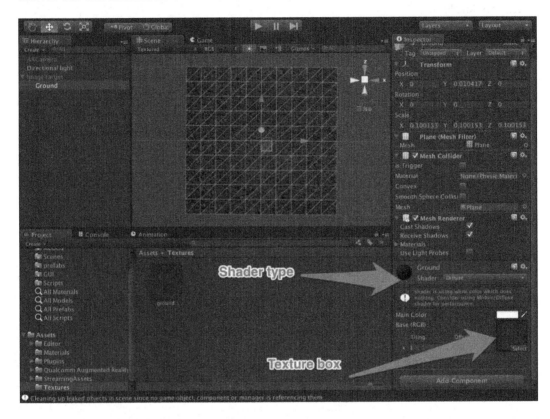

Now we have an ok looking ground for our moles. Notice that the shader for the material is **Diffuse**. This type of shader is suitable for opaque materials and works perfectly fine for the ground texture. Later on, we can use different shaders for different materials to achieve different results, such as the transparency or particle shader.

The Whack-A-Mole model

Now that we have the ground to build on, it is time to add our mole model to the project. Simply create a folder in the **Assets** folder, and name it Models. Drag-and-drop the file from the chapter assets named WhackAMoleModel.fbx. Unity will automatically import the model into the project and will create a prefab for us.

1. Like we have done before, drag-and-drop the prefab created for WhackAMoleModel into our scene. You might not automatically see where the model was added; this is mainly because the model is too small in comparison to the ground plane. If you focus on the model by holding the *F* key, you will see how small the model is.

To change that, we can scale the model using the same way we did before, which is to scale it from the editor, or we can change the FBX Converter settings. The FBX Converter settings handle how the model is inserted into our scene through many settings specific to the model. If we are to scale the model in the editor, it will naturally not have a 1:1 ratio between the model and the world. This is done in real time, takes up resources, and makes scripting more confusing and frustrating. It is recommend to scale objects from their model settings.

2. Click on the model's prefab in the folder, and the **Inspector** will display the **FBX Converter** settings. There is a setting for **Scale Factor**, that is by default set to a very small value, which is **0.01**. This is how big the model is to be inserted to the scene compared to its original scale from the 3D modeling application. Change this setting to **0.7**, and click on **Apply**. The model will resize automatically in the scene without changing the scale transform in the scene itself. The following screenshot shows WhackAMoleModel scaled and positioned in the middle:

3. Position the model exactly at the center of the ground and to be on top of the ground correctly. After that, attach the **WhackAMoleModel** object to the **ImageTarget** in the **Hierarchy** to set the **ImageTarget** as its parent object.

Adding colliders to the scene

Unity simulates physics for the objects in the game, but only when we specify what is being simulated and how. The reason for this is that in most games, not every single object is simulated by physics. For example, not every wall in every game is breakable. There are static objects that are just there simply defying physics, but for games, that is quite all right.

Collider is a component that we can attach to any object in the scene that makes this object "collidable" with any other collidable object. For example, if we are making a shooting game such as *Call of Duty* or the likes of it, if we do not attach a collider to all walls in our game, the game character will be able to simple "walk through" the wall. This is, of course, not desirable.

For our game, we need to be able to "whack" the mole; if there is no collider on the mole, we certainly won't be able to whack it. Also, the balls that we will be shooting at the moles need to be able to collide with the ground, not just pass through it. All of this is possible with colliders.

1. First, select the **WhackAMoleModel** from the scene, and expand it to reveal the **MoleHill** and the character. Those are the two components to which we need to add the colliders. First, select the character from the scene, and select **Box Collider** by navigating to **Component | Physics**. This will add a collider with the shape of a box around the character. The box won't be exactly wrapping the character, but it is cheap on resources, and is enough in our case to simulate a good collision with the balls that we will fire at the moles.

2. Next, select the **MoleHill**; the **MoleHill** is irregular in shape, and we need the ball collision with it to be simulated more effectively than what a box collider can do. This is why we need to use a Mesh collider. From the same previous menu, now choose **Mesh Collider** to be added to the **MoleHill** model. What the **Mesh Collider** does is that it adds a collider that is exactly the same shape as the model on top of it, so it simulates the collision exactly the same as the model.

The following screenshot shows colliders added to the **Mole** model:

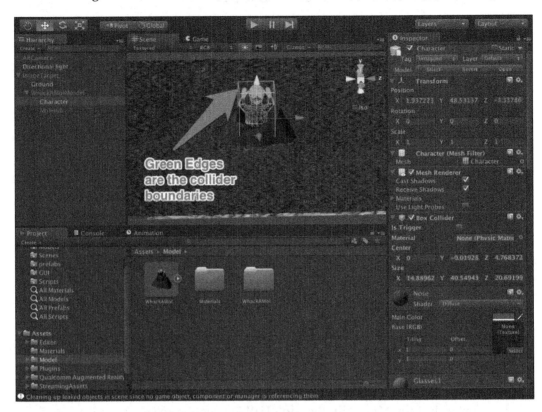

Notice that the ground already has a collider added to it. That is because, by default, any primitive object created in the editor has a collider attached to it.

Creating the ball for the ball gun

Now that we have the general feeling of the game being set, we need to create the gun's projectile. It is understandable that because it's a ball gun, it will just shoot spheres, which we can create through a script. But before we can do that, we need a role model for the script to clone and create in the scene. So, the next thing we will work on is creating the basis for the gun's projectile prefab.

1. Select **ARCamera** from the **Hierarchy** panel, and then from the **GameObject** menu navigate to **Create | Other | Sphere**. This will create a sphere where **ARCamera** is; however, it will not parent it to the camera. It is particularly useful when creating objects at the position of other objects. Change the name of the sphere we just created to Ball.

2. Now, the main idea is to have the projectile occupy at least half the camera's view and be at the center of it to give the user a sense of immersion while shooting the balls at the moles. This is easily achievable with everything we know. Simply position the ball directly in front of the camera and resize it till you feel its size is appropriate to the camera. We can check how big it will look like if we look at the **Game** panel in the editor or **Camera Preview** at the bottom-right corner of the **Scene** panel when selecting the camera.

3. Once the position and scale is right, create a material in the **Materials** folder, and name it `ball`. When selecting this material, in the Inspector you will notice a color box that is by default set to **white**. For the ball, we do not need a texture like we did for the ground, but rather, just a color that will make it contrast over the environment. So, just set the color box to red, and then attach the material to the ball. The following screenshot shows the **Ball** projectile in the **Scene** panel:

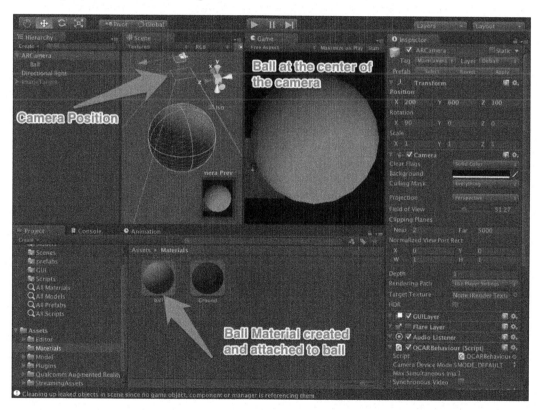

Notice that the ball already has a collider by default, which will come in handy when we want the ball to actually collide with the moles and the ground.

There is one fundamental thing to point out; adding a collider to the object doesn't make it simulated by physics in the engine, it only makes it collidable with other colliders. But of course, we want the projectile to act like a real projectile and respond to gravity and forces. We want the projectile to bounce off of the floor and off of the moles in a natural way. This is easily simulated in Unity, but we need to tell Unity what to simulate and how.

Select the **ball** object from the **Hierarchy** panel, and from **Components** menu, go to **Physics**, and select **Rigidbody**. This adds a Rigidbody component to the ball. What the Rigidbody component does is that it simulates physics on the object it is attached to as if the object is a rigid body in the real world. It simulates gravity, bounce, external forces, and everything to which you would expect a real-world rigid body be subjected to, such as an air drag.

By default, the Rigidbody component is set to simulate gravity on the object. We do not need to change any settings in Rigidbody because they all suit us for now. Simply click the Play button, and we will immediately see the ball falling down in the game world under the effect of gravity.

Setting global gravity settings

We might have noticed that the ball was falling a little too slow for it to feel natural for the game. This is mainly because our scale is not 1:1 with the game. It is rather 1:1 with the real world. This is because it is an AR application, and the concern is for it to feel natural with the real-world interaction. This, however, makes us all giants in comparison to the game world when using the AR game. So, it's not that the ball that is falling too slow, a bit of Einstein's relativity coming, it's that the ball that is falling a great distance in relation to us.

To remedy that, we need to bring up the force of gravity to compensate for the giant status in which we are located. If the gravity is stronger, the ball will fall faster and will give us the feeling that it is natural for our own real world. Luckily, changing the gravity setting in a Unity project is quite simple.

1. From the **Edit** menu, go to **Project** settings, and select **Physics**. In the **Inspector**, we will be presented with a number of settings all related to how physics works. We can change any of them, but we only need one changed for now. The first setting is related to gravity. Gravity in the real world acts on the y axis and is roughly -9.81 in magnitude. We need this to be 6 times stronger, so change it to `-60.81`.

2. Click on the Run button, and watch the ball fall much faster and in a more natural manner. The following screenshot shows the gravity settings for the project:

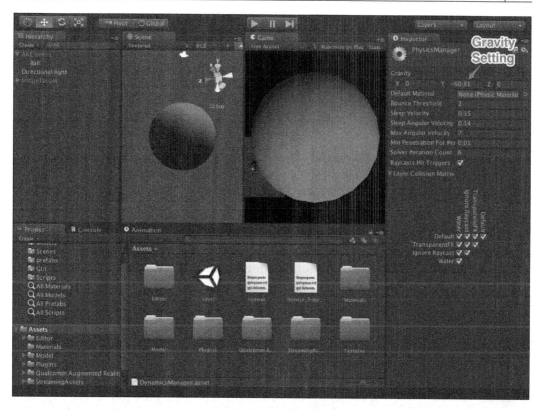

This should take care of the physics compensation value and should work naturally in the real world in an AR environment.

Adding audio sources

We now need to create sound sources in the scene to handle sound effects for the game. **Sound sources** are audio sources that can be position in the world for 3D positional sound or simple 2D sounds. In order to hear sound effects in the game, audio sources are needed to produce the sound, but also we need a listener to actually capture the created sound to present to the user.

By default, **ARCamera** has a listener component added to it, so we only need to add the audio sources to it.

1. Create a folder and name it Audio in the **Assets** folder. Drag-and-drop the two files inside the **Audio** folder in the chapter's assets. This will import the two audio files named ballFire.wav and moleHit.wav. We will use the first for the sound effect of firing the ball from the gun, and the second for when a ball hits a mole.

    Because this is an arcade game, we do not need 3D sound positions; we mostly need all audio to be 2D and independent of how far or close we are to the sound source. We do this by changing the setting for the audio assets, which we just imported, in the Inspector.

2. Select the audio file from the **Audio** folder, and from the **Inspector** uncheck the checkbox named **3D Sound**. Do the same for both files. The following screenshot shows the audio settings for the audio files:

3. Now, select **ARCamera**, and then from the **GameObject** menu, select **Create Empty**. What this does is it creates an empty object in the world and near **ARCamera**. Now, rename the object to `ballFireAudio`. Now, select the object we have just created, and from the **Component** menu, navigate to **Audio | Audio source**. Repeat the same steps to create `moleHitAudio`.

4. Drag-and-drop the audio file from the **Audio** folder appropriately into the audio source component we have just created. This effectively creates sound sources in our scene. Just uncheck the checkbox named **Play on Awake**, because we need to control this audio source through code. It is a useful option to test how the sound source will play out in the game panel though. The following screenshot shows sound source settings for **ballFireAudio**:

Now that the sound sources are in place, we can easily call on them from script to add to the immersion of the app.

Scripting the ball gun

We have already created the projectile for the gun, and we also created the sound source for it, but we are yet to make this act like a ball gun; this is when scripting comes in handy.

The first thing we need to do is to create a prefab for the projectile we created. This is to be able to clone the projectile through the script and fire it at the poor moles. To do that, simply create a folder in the **Assets** folder, and name it Prefabs. Drag-and-drop the **Ball** object from the **Hierarchy** panel to the folder you just created. Now we have a prefab that we can call upon through code and can create as many balls as we want.

The ball we have attached to the camera is meaningless, because we will be creating the projectiles through code. So, after we have already made a prefab of the ball, we no longer need it in the scene, but before we remove that, there is another step. We need to have a placeholder from which the projectiles spawn. That placeholder should be in the same position and with the same rotation as the ball we have in the scene right now.

First, we add an empty object to the scene from the **GameObject** menu. Now, attach that object to the **ARCamera** object by dragging-and-dropping it. Rename that object to BallPlaceHolder. We need the BallPlaceHolder object to have the exact same transformation as that of the **Ball** object. Unfortunately, there is no automatic function in Unity that copies the transformation for two objects, so we need to manually copy it. Click the **Ball** object and copy both the position and rotation of that object, and insert them into the BallPlaceHolder object. Then, delete the **Ball** object, because we no longer need it.

The following screenshot shows **BallPlaceHolder** added to the scene:

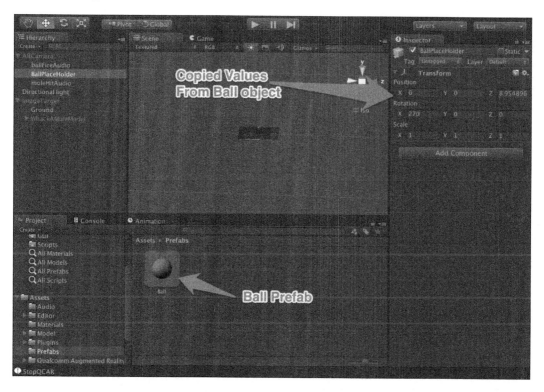

Now, it is time to create a folder for our scripts. Create a new folder in **Assets**, and rename it **Scripts**. Inside the **Scripts** folder, from **Assets** menu, navigate to **Create | C# Script**. Name the created file `ballGun`. Now, double-click on it, and Unity will automatically open its MonoDevelop Editor for us.

The following screenshot shows the Unity MonoDevelop Editor:

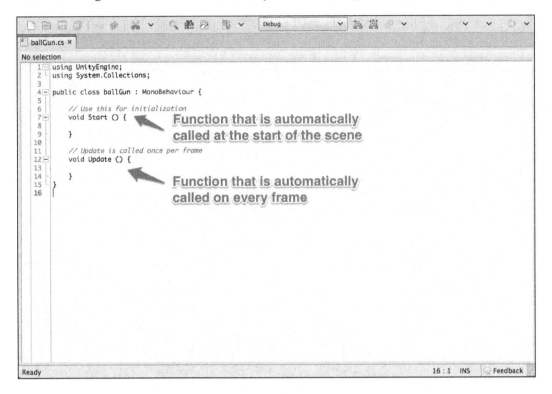

Unity automatically creates a number of things for us in the MonoDevelop Editor. First, it creates a class template with the name of the script file. This is why the script filename must be that of the class name, among other reasons. It adds two empty functions for us that are very crucial to game development on the platform.

The Start() function is a function that is called automatically by Unity engine when the scene starts. It is very useful for variable initialization, and can be thought of as the constructor for the class.

The Update() function is a very important function that Unity automatically calls on every frame that passes in the game. This is very important for keeping track of the game object state, maintaining game logic, and many other uses. It is strongly advised not to have intensive calculations inside the Update() function, because it will slow down the frame rates of the game, because Unity doesn't render the next frame till all Update() functions in the game are executed completely.

Now, let's look at the script after the code has been added to it and see what every function does. The following screenshot shows the `ballGun.cs` script:

```
ballGun.cs ×
ballGun > projectilePlaceHolder
1   using UnityEngine;
2   using System.Collections;
3
4   public class ballGun : MonoBehaviour {
5
6       public GameObject projectile;
7       public Transform projectilePlaceHolder;
8       private GameObject ballFireAudio;
9
10      private GameObject Trackable;
11
12      // Use this for initialization
13      void Start () {
14          ballFireAudio = this.gameObject.transform.FindChild("ballFireAudio").gameObject;
15          Trackable = GameObject.Find("ImageTarget").gameObject;
16      }
17
18      // Update is called once per frame
19      void Update () {
20          if(Input.GetMouseButtonDown(0))
21          {
22              ballFireAudio.audio.Play();
23              GameObject obj = Instantiate(projectile,
24                  projectilePlaceHolder.position,
25                  this.gameObject.transform.rotation) as GameObject;
26              obj.gameObject.rigidbody.AddRelativeForce(Vector3.forward * Time.deltaTime * 1100000);
27              obj.transform.parent = Trackable.transform;
28              Destroy(obj.gameObject,5f);
29          }
30      }
31  }
32
```

This is how the script that will control the behavior of the ball gun appears. We will be attaching this script to the ARCamera object, and it will respond to user's touch anywhere on the screen to fire a ball directly toward where the user is pointing the camera. Let's see what every function does in this script.

The first things we see are the declared variables for the script. They follow a similar syntax to what you would expect from a C# language:

```
public GameObject projectile;
public Transform projectilePlaceHolder;
private GameObject ballFireAudio;
private Gameobject Trackable;
```

The `public` or `private` status of the variable is very important in Unity. This is because `public` variables appear in the Editor, and their values can be set in the **Inspector**. This is particularly useful and should be kept in mind.

The `projectile` variable is what we will use from which to link to the **Ball** prefab. It is `public`, because we will set its value from the Editor, as we will see in a little while. `projectile` is of type `GameObject`, which is the general type for any object in the game. It contains a large number of relevant functions and variables that often come in handy. wer sadfas

The variable `projectilePlaceHolder` is of type `Transform`. It will hold the transform information of the `BallPlaceHolder` object we have in the scene on which to spawn projectiles.

For the variable `ballFireAudio`, as its name suggests, we will be using this to link to the audio source object we created earlier.

The `Trackable` variable will be used to link to the `ImageTarget` object. We will use it to parent the spawned projectiles to it. We will do that to allow the balls to disappear if `Trackable` is lost from sight:

```
void Start() {
    ballFireAudio = this.gameObject.transform.
FindChild("ballFireAudio").gameObject;
    Trackable = GameObject.Find("ImageTarget").gameObject;
}
```

This is how our `Start()` function looks like. In this function, we are initializing both `ballFireAudio` and `Trackable` variables. We do that by finding the `GameObject` from the scene and attaching it to the variable. Notice that we find the `GameObject` by its name; if the name is different, change it accordingly, or the variable will not be initialized correctly:

```
void Update () {
    if(Input.GetMouseButtonDown(0))
    {
        ballFireAudio.audio.Play();
        GameObject obj = Instantiate(projectile,
            projectilePlaceHolder.position,
            this.gameObject.transform.rotation) as GameObject;
        obj.gameObject.rigidbody.AddRelativeForce(Vector3.forward *
Time.deltaTime * 1100000);
        obj.transform.parent = Trackable.transform;
        Destroy(obj.gameObject,5f);
    }
}
```

This is our `Update()` function that will be called with every frame. It mainly listens for user interaction; if the user touches the screen or clicks with the mouse, a **Ball** prefab is instantiated and a force is applied on it to propel it forward with a sound effect. Repeated clicks or touches will spawn more balls.

What `Input.GetMouseButtonDown(0)` does is that it returns `true` if the user clicks with the mouse or touches the screen. This is how we listen if the user interacted with the screen. If it is `true`, we proceed with our game logic.

We first play the audio attached to the game object `ballFireAudio` to play the sound effect for ball shooting.

Next, we instantiate a new clone from the prefab **Ball** attached to a projectile variable. We instantiate it into the variable `obj` with the transform of the `projectilePlaceHolder` position and the rotation of the camera so that it always fires forward.

We then apply the relative force to the instantiated object's `Rigidbody` component to fire forward. The direction is `Vector3.forward`, which is the object's forward direction. We multiply it by `Time.deltaTime`; we do this to make the force frame rate independent (`Time.deltaTime` is the time since the last frame). This avoids making the ball slower if the frame rate drops down for any reason. Then we multiply by the force's power. Notice that the force is really big; this is because we need the ball to fire forward quickly and to also compensate for the ratio between the game world and the real world as we saw with gravity.

We then parent the instantiated object to `ImageTarget` so that it behaves correctly with the image target.

Finally, we destroy the object with a delay of 5 seconds. We do that because we do not ever want projectiles to disappear, as this will really deteriorate the performance of the app.

1. Now that our script is ready, we need to attach it to the **ARCamera** object. Do this by dragging the script and dropping it on the **ARCamera** object. The script component will appear in **ARCamera** and we will notice that the two public variables **Projectile** and **Projectile Place Holder** are visible in the **Inspector**.

2. Now, we need to drag-and-drop the **Ball** prefab from the **Prefabs** folder to the **Projectile** variable in the **Inspector**. We also need to drag-and-drop the **BallPlaceHolder** object from the scene to the variable **Projectile Place Holder** variable in the **Inspector**. The following shows **ARCamera** with the `ballGun.cs` script attached:

3. Now that our script is attached correctly to our **ARCamera** object, we can now try it out in the **Game** view. Click on Run and the click over the panel. The camera will shoot out balls. The following screenshot shows the `ballGun.cs` script in action:

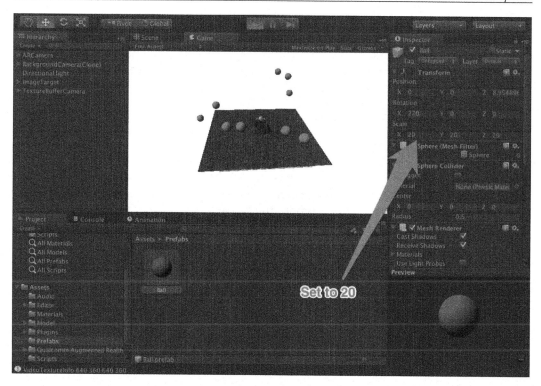

Set to 20

4. On testing the script, we might notice that the balls are a little too small in comparison to the mole. We can change that through the **Ball** prefab direction from the **Prefabs** folder. Select it, and then change the scale value for (x, y, z) to 20. This is a prime example of how useful prefabs are when doing changes, because it automatically propagates it for the project.

Vuforia trackable event handler

More often than not, we need to attach a certain behavior that triggers when a trackable is found. To do this, we must understand how to keep a track of trackable events, such as trackable found or trackable lost. Vuforia makes this easy for us by providing a template script named `DefaultTrackableEventHandler`. This script is by default attached to any **ImageTarget** prefab. It should be there now in our **ImageTarget** object in the scene.

What the script does is it handles the event of a trackable found or a trackable lost. It is the script responsible for rendering the 3D content when the trackable is found, and making it disappear when it is lost as well. It is important to notice that it is however not responsible for the perspective or the **ARCamera** position on the trackable, this is handled by another script , which is beyond our scope.

Vuforia recommends that we create our own trackable event handler scripts using the `DefaultTrackableEventHandler` script as a template. This is exactly what we will do now by adding a very small function to the script.

Open the script named `DefaultTrackableEventHandler`, which can be found inside the `Scripts` folder under the `Qualcomm Augmented reality` folder. It should look similar to the following screenshot, where the `DefaultTrackableEventHandler.cs` script is shown:

```
DefaultTrackableEventHandler.cs
No selection                                                                          No region
  1 /* ... */
  6
  7  using UnityEngine;
  8
  9  /// A custom handler that implements the ITrackableEventHandler ...
 12  public class DefaultTrackableEventHandler : MonoBehaviour,
 13                                              ITrackableEventHandler
 14  {
 15      #region PRIVATE_MEMBER_VARIABLES
 16
 17      private TrackableBehaviour mTrackableBehaviour;
 18
 19      #endregion // PRIVATE_MEMBER_VARIABLES
 20
 21
 22
 23      #region UNTIY_MONOBEHAVIOUR_METHODS
 24
 25      void Start()
 26      {
 27          mTrackableBehaviour = GetComponent<TrackableBehaviour>();
 28          if (mTrackableBehaviour)
 29          {
 30              mTrackableBehaviour.RegisterTrackableEventHandler(this);
 31          }
 32
 33          OnTrackingLost();
 34      }
 35
 36      #endregion // UNTIY_MONOBEHAVIOUR_METHODS
 37
 38
 39
 40      #region PUBLIC_METHODS
 41
 42      /// Implementation of the ITrackableEventHandler...
 46      public void OnTrackableStateChanged(
 47                          TrackableBehaviour.Status previousStatus,
 48                          TrackableBehaviour.Status newStatus)
 49      {
 50          if (newStatus == TrackableBehaviour.Status.DETECTED ||
 51              newStatus == TrackableBehaviour.Status.TRACKED)
 52          {
 53              OnTrackingFound();
 54          }
 55          else
 56          {
 57              OnTrackingLost();
 58          }
 59      }
 60
 61      #endregion // PUBLIC_METHODS
 62
```

The following three functions are important to understand from this script:

- OnTrackableStateChanged: This function is called every time the state of the trackable is changed, whether it is found or lost. It then determines if it is detected or lost, and appropriately calls on the event function.

- OnTrackingFound: This is the function that is called when the trackable is found. It is responsible for rendering all the children of the ImageTarget object and switching on their colliders.

- OnTrackingLost: This function is called when the trackable is lost. It is responsible for turning off the rendering for all the child objects of ImageTarget. It also turns off the collider for them.

These are the three crucial functions in the script. We will leave them as they are for our app, but for one modification. We need to add a new function that returns the status of the trackable to tell us whether the trackable is detected or not. This will be useful for us when animating the mole character, as we will see in a little while.

Create a new C# script in the Scripts folder and name it MoleTrackableEventHandler. Now copy all the code from the script DefaultTrackableEventHandler and paste it inside the script we just created. It is important to change the class name from DefaultTrackableEventHandler to MoleTrackableEventHandler, else errors will appear in Unity due to the fact that the class name is not the same as the filename.

After modification, the script will look similar to the following screenshot, where the `MoleTrackableEventHandler.cs` script is shown:

```
1 ⊞  /*  ...                                                          */
6
7    using UnityEngine;
8
9 ⊞  /// A custom handler that implements the ITrackableEventHandler ...
12   public class MoleTrackableEventHandler : MonoBehaviour,          ◄— Change the name to
13                                   ITrackableEventHandler               MoleTrackbleEventHandler
14   {
15 ⊟     #region PRIVATE_MEMBER_VARIABLES
16
17        private TrackableBehaviour mTrackableBehaviour;
18
19        private bool TrackableStatus=false;                          ◄— Added Variable
20                                                                        TrackableStatus
21        #endregion // PRIVATE_MEMBER_VARIABLES
22
23 ⊟     #region UNTIY_MONOBEHAVIOUR_METHODS
24
25 ⊟     void Start()
26        {
27           mTrackableBehaviour = GetComponent<TrackableBehaviour>();
28           if (mTrackableBehaviour)
29           {
30              mTrackableBehaviour.RegisterTrackableEventHandler(this);
31           }
32
33           OnTrackingLost();
34        }
35
36        #endregion // UNTIY_MONOBEHAVIOUR_METHODS
37
38 ⊟     #region PUBLIC_METHODS
39
40 ⊞     /// Implementation of the ITrackableEventHandler...
44        public void OnTrackableStateChanged(
45                          TrackableBehaviour.Status previousStatus,
46 ⊟                        TrackableBehaviour.Status newStatus)
47        {
48           if (newStatus == TrackableBehaviour.Status.DETECTED ||
49              newStatus == TrackableBehaviour.Status.TRACKED)
50           {
51              TrackableStatus = true;                                ◄— Set to true when found
52              OnTrackingFound();
53           }
54           else
55           {                                                         ◄— Set to false when lost
56              TrackableStatus = false;
57              OnTrackingLost();
58           }
59        }
60        //Returns true if the trackable is visible. False otherwise.
61 ⊟     public bool trackableVisible(){                               ◄— Function to check if
62           return TrackableStatus;                                      the Trackable is visible
63        }
64
```

We added the variable `TrackableStatus`, which we want to hold the state of the trackable. It will be `true` if it is visible, and `false` if not. We then created a function and named it `trackableVisible`, which will return the variable `TrackableStatus`.

We then simply set the `TrackableStatus` to `true` when found and `false` when not found inside the function `OnTrackableStateChanged()`.

Now, if we call on the function `trackableVisible()`; it will effectively tell us if the trackable is visible or not.

Now, we need to attach the `MoleTrackableEventHandler` to the `ImageTarget` object in our scene. We now do not need `DefaultTrackableEventHandler` attached to `ImageTarget`, so we need to delete that component or simply disable it.

`DefaultTrackabeEventHandler` can be customized later on for all sorts of effects such as playing a sound or video when the trackable is found, or controlling specific GUI objects to respond to the trackable. It gives us a lot of control over the behavior of the AR app, so it always pays off to keep it in mind.

Adding a Particles prefab

Particles in Unity is a very useful tool that many developers use. With it, it is possible to create fog, dust, flames, explosions, and all sorts of effects. The effect on resources is usually minimal, as Particles uses small 2D images animated to give the effect needed, hence the name Particles.

For our app, it will be useful to add dust particles appear when we whack the mole with the balls fired at them. Although learning how to create particles is outside the scope of this book, we will see how we can add one to the scene that is already made, because there are a number of free particles available through the Unity store.

1. Import the package named `DustParticles` to the project. Add the prefab we just imported to the scene. You will automatically notice the dust cloud being simulated in the Editor. Now, we only need to position it appropriately over the molehill and have it look as if the dust is rising from the hold, then parent it to the Mole object. In a little while, we will see how we can call on this particle system and activated it through code.

2. Change the position of the **Character** object to be under the ground, because this is where they should be when the game starts. It will also give us a good idea how the dust will look like with character not present. Simply move the Character on the y axis till it is just below the ground and not visible. The following screenshot shows dust particles added to the scene:

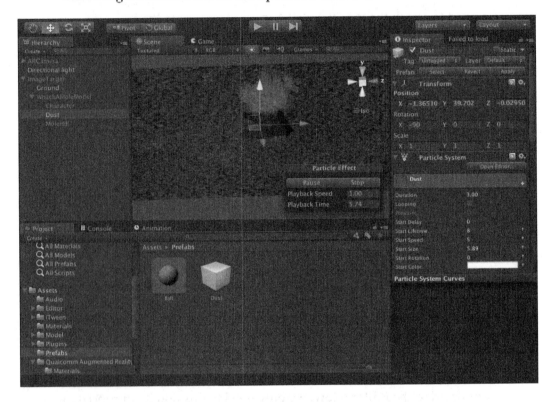

Unity is a great tool, but like everything else, it is not perfect. What it lacks, however, is usually remedied by a very active community that create add-ons and scripts for it. One of the most useful and free scripts available for Unity is iTween.

iTween is a script that allows us to animate objects quite easily through script. It is very customizable, and fits most object animation needs for games. For example, iTween can easily be used to animate a missile in a game to home at the target in a fluid manner. In our case, we will use iTween to animate the mole coming out of the molehill and going back.

iTween can be easily added from the Unity's Asset store. It is for free; simply search for it in the Unity Asset store, which is accessible from the **Window** menu, then download and import into the project. Now, we can access iTween functions easily from code.

iTween's documentations can be found at `http://itween.pixelplacement.com/documentation.php`.

Scripting the mole character

Now that iTween is in place, let's see how we can script the mole character to make use of iTween and animate the character correctly. What we are aiming to achieve with the mole script at this stage is to have it animate up and down from the molehill. The animation should start at a random time between two ranges to avoid repetition and predictability of the behavior.

Let's take a look at how this script looks like. The following screenshot shows `moleAnimator.cs` script:

```
moleAnimator.cs  ×
moleAnimator >  Start ()
 1    using UnityEngine;
 2    using System.Collections;
 3
 4    public class moleAnimator : MonoBehaviour {
 5
 6        private ParticleSystem dust;
 7        private GameObject moleHitAudio;
 8        private MoleTrackableEventHandler trackableHandler;
 9
10        // Use this for initialization
11        void Start () {
12            moleHitAudio = GameObject.Find("ARCamera").transform.FindChild("moleHitAudio").gameObject;
13            dust = this.gameObject.transform.parent.transform.FindChild("Dust").
14                gameObject.GetComponent<ParticleSystem>();
15            trackableHandler = GameObject.Find("ImageTarget").gameObject.GetComponent<MoleTrackableEventHandler>();
16
17            iTween.MoveBy(gameObject, iTween.Hash("y", 40, "easeType", "easeInOutQuad","speed",20,
18                "delay", Random.Range(0.3f,5f), "oncomplete","animComplete_Up"));
19        }
20
21        //Function called when animation below ground is complete
22        public void animComplete_Down()
23        {
24            //Only make the mole character visible if the Tackable is visible. This is to avoid having the
25            //mole character visible with no detected Trackable
26            if(trackableHandler.trackableVisible())
27            {
28                this.gameObject.renderer.enabled=true;
29                this.gameObject.collider.enabled=true;
30            }
31
32            iTween.MoveBy(gameObject, iTween.Hash("y", 40, "easeType", "easeInOutQuad","speed",20,
33                "delay",Random.Range(0.3f,5f), "oncomplete","animComplete_Up"));
34        }
35
36        //Function called when animation above ground is complete
37        public void animComplete_Up()
38        {
39            iTween.MoveBy(gameObject, iTween.Hash("y", -40, "easeType", "easeInOutQuad","speed",20,
40                "delay",Random.Range(0.3f,1f), "oncomplete","animComplete_Down"));
41        }
42
43        void OnCollisionEnter(Collision collision) {
44            dust.Play();
45            moleHitAudio.audio.Play();
46            this.gameObject.renderer.enabled=false;
47            this.gameObject.collider.enabled=false;
48        }
49    }
50

Ready                                                          13 : 74  INS      Feedback
```

The first three lines in the `Start()` function are quite simple. We find and attach the mole hit sound source to `moleHitAudio` to be used by us in the script. We find and attach the dust particle system to use as a hit effect. We then find the `ImageTarget` object and only use the script component `MoleTrackableEventHandler`. We do this to be able to call on the function that added, which is `trackableVisible`, to check to see if the trackable is visible or not. This is one way of accessing other class' functions in Unity.

The last line in the `Start()` function starts the animation sequence; let's see how it does it:

```
iTween.MoveBy(gameObject, iTween.Hash("y", 40, "easeType",
"easeInOutQuad", "speed", 20, "delay", Random.Range(0.3f, 5f),
"oncomplete", "animComplete_Up");
```

This is the line of code that starts the whole animation sequence on the mole character. `MoveBy()` is a function in the iTween class that allows animating objects in a given axis by moving them along it. We first give it the current game object to which the script is attached, which will be the mole character, and then we pass in the `iTween.Hash` parameters to set what kind of animation we want.

The parameters for `iTween.Hash` are very important, but easy to understand. It follows the syntax of (`parameter name string, parameter value`). First, we give it the actual axis on which we want to animate, which is in our case y axis. Then, we set a value for `easyType`, which governs the slowing down and speeding up of the animation to make it not feel abrupt; `easeInOutQuad` is a perfect natural feel for our character. We set the speed of the animation to `20`. Now for the delay, which is the delay of the animation start, we add a random value to make moles animate at different times, and not all at the same time, because we will have more than one mole in our scene at a later stage. The `oncomplete` parameter is the name of the function to be called once the animation is complete. Because this line animates the character up and out of the hole, it calls on `animComplete_up`, which in turn will animate the character back down and into the hole, as we will see next.

If we look at the function `animComplete_Up`, we will see that it only contains a single line of code that does something similar to what the `Start()` function did in its last code line, but reversed. It animates the character back down and into the hole, which makes sense, because we want the character to not pop up and down from the molehill. Notice that the `oncomplete` parameter calls on `animComplete_Down`, which we will take a look at next.

In function `animComplete_Down`, we do two things. First we check to see if the trackable is visible by calling the `trackableVisible()` function, which is a member of `MoleTrackableEventHandler`. If the target is visible, we turn on `renderer` and `collider` for the object. This makes the object visible and collidable. We do this because we will make the mole disappear when the ball hits it, but we should only make it reappear if the trackable is visible, otherwise it will interfere with how `ImageTarget` renders objects, and we will see floating objects on the camera when there is no tracked target. Next, it animates the object back up and then `oncomplete` in turn calls `animComplete_Up`, making a perfect recursive loop.

The last function, which is `OnCollisionEnter`, is a Unity event that fires up whenever two colliders collide with each other. It is sent to any object with a collider attached to it. We use this event to check if any ball hit the mole or not. If it does hit the mole, we then play the hit sound and the dust particles. We then turn off the renderer of the object to make it disappear and turn off the collider to not interfere with any more balls.

This is the script that will handle the mole behavior for us. Now all we have to do is attach it to the `Character` object inside the `WhackAMoleModel` object and hit Play. We can immediately see the mole is animating correctly and randomly. Also, if a ball hits it, sound effects and dust particles are played, indicating a correct whack.

Now as our mole object is complete, prefab the whole object into the `Prefabs` folder and then add multiple mole objects into the scene to have more than one mole. Add as many as you would want, but I believe four is a good enough number, considering how small the trackable is.

Mask shader

We are mostly done with the game. We have the behavior of all our objects in place and are ready for deployment; but we are missing one last thing. We might have noticed that when the moles go underground, they are still visible from the side angle. This will be apparent as well when deploying the app to the device in AR environment. There is an easy solution we can do to hide those moles when they go underground in an AR environment, which is using a depth mask shader.

1. Add the shader asset named `DepthMask.shader`, which can be found in the chapter's assets. Then, we want to create a cube in our scene that will be as big as the ground plane and name it `mask`, and hide all the moles behind it, as shown in the following screenshot. The following screenshot also shows the **Mask** object added to scene:

2. Of course, this object is not acting as a mask yet, it is just an ordinary cube. To give it the mask properties, we need to create a material for it in the **Materials** folder and name it `Mask`. Because we added the **DepthMask** shader, it should be automatically available in the **Shader** dropdown list for the material. Simply choose the **DepthMask** shader from there, and then attach the material to the **Mask** object. The following screenshot shows the **DepthMask** shader activated:

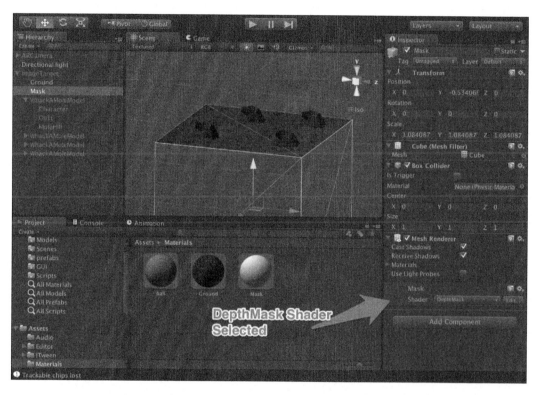

We immediately notice that the cube has disappeared, but further inspection reveals that not only the cube is not visible, but also the moles behind it. This effectively fixes our problem by hiding the moles underground.

Summary

In this chapter we covered a lot of ground on the advanced AR development in Unity. We created a perfectly functional and fun game that utilizes a lot of concepts in both Unity and Vuforia. All we need to do now is deploy the game to a device and play with it. Maybe add a score system, or maybe add a limited number of balls to hit the mole. The sky is your limit. Experiment with it, and create an experience that users will appreciate.

Index

image targets
creating 61-65
feature distribution 73
patterns 76, 77
trackables 61
immersion factor
used, for content delivery 8, 9
Inspector (Inspector panel) 22
Inspector panel 32
installations
Unity 3D 17, 18
Vuforia 19
iOS
deploying for, in build settings 35-37
iTween 108

M

mask shader 112, 113
mole character
scripting 109-111
MoveBy() function 110
Multi-Targets 11

O

OnTrackableStateChanged functions 105
OnTrackingFound functions 105
OnTrackingLost functions 105

P

packages
importing, in Unity project 23-26
packages, importing in Unity project
trackable files 27-29
Unity scene files 24-26
particles 107
Particles prefab
adding 107, 108
prefab, Vuforia
3D objects, attaching 49-57
3D objects, importing 49-57
about 41-48
Directional Light, adding to scene 56
Hierarchy panel 57
object, positioning 44

projectile variable 100
Project (Project assets) panel 22

R

Resolution and Presentation settings 36

S

scene files, in Unity files 24-26
Show Features link 69
smartphones
Augmented reality (AR) 7, 8
Start() function 111
Switch Platform button 32, 35

T

Target Manager 61
Texture property 86
trackable event handler
in Vuforia 103-105
trackables
about 61
in image targets 61
trackable score
augmentability 66
deciding, factors 66-69
enhancing, by contrast enhancement 71, 72
featues, Target Manager 70
trackableVisible() function 111
tracking solutions components, Vuforia
SDK
about 12, 13
ARCamera 10
Image Target 10
Virtual Button 11, 12

U

Unity
as game engine 82
datasets, exporting to 78, 79
supported formats 49
Unity 3D
downloading 17
installing 17

integrating, with Vuforia 14, 15
website 18
Unity, as game engine
about 82
environment, setting up 82, 83
Unity Editor 79
Unity objects
parenting 58
Unity project
creating, Vuforia used 39-41
packages, importing 23
starting 21
Unity scenes 21, 22
Update() function 101

V

Virtual Button 11
Vuforia
downloading 18, 20
installing 18, 20
prefab 41

sample apps 20
sample projects 20, 21
trackable event handler 103-106
Unity 3D, integrating with 14, 15
used, for Unity project creating 39-41
Vuforia SDK Unity extension 19
Vuforia SDK
about 9
tracking solutions components 10, 11

W

Whack-A-Mole game
about 83
ground level, creating 84-86
Whack-A-Mole model
about 87
colliders, adding to scene 89, 90

Z

Z-Buffer conflict 85

Thank you for buying
Developing AR Games for iOS And Android

About Packt Publishing

Packt, pronounced 'packed', published its first book "*Mastering phpMyAdmin for Effective MySQL Management*" in April 2004 and subsequently continued to specialize in publishing highly focused books on specific technologies and solutions.

Our books and publications share the experiences of your fellow IT professionals in adapting and customizing today's systems, applications, and frameworks. Our solution based books give you the knowledge and power to customize the software and technologies you're using to get the job done. Packt books are more specific and less general than the IT books you have seen in the past. Our unique business model allows us to bring you more focused information, giving you more of what you need to know, and less of what you don't.

Packt is a modern, yet unique publishing company, which focuses on producing quality, cutting-edge books for communities of developers, administrators, and newbies alike. For more information, please visit our website: www.packtpub.com.

About Packt Open Source

In 2010, Packt launched two new brands, Packt Open Source and Packt Enterprise, in order to continue its focus on specialization. This book is part of the Packt Open Source brand, home to books published on software built around Open Source licences, and offering information to anybody from advanced developers to budding web designers. The Open Source brand also runs Packt's Open Source Royalty Scheme, by which Packt gives a royalty to each Open Source project about whose software a book is sold.

Writing for Packt

We welcome all inquiries from people who are interested in authoring. Book proposals should be sent to author@packtpub.com. If your book idea is still at an early stage and you would like to discuss it first before writing a formal book proposal, contact us; one of our commissioning editors will get in touch with you.

We're not just looking for published authors; if you have strong technical skills but no writing experience, our experienced editors can help you develop a writing career, or simply get some additional reward for your expertise.

Unity Game Development Essentials

ISBN: 978-1-84719-818-1   Paperback: 316 pages

Build fully functional, professional 3D games with realistic environments, sound, dynamics effects, and more!

1. Kick start game development, and build ready-to-play 3D games with ease

2. Understand key concepts in game design including scripting, physics, instantiation, particle effects, and more

3. Test & optimize your game to perfection with essential tips-and-tricks

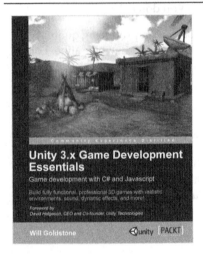

Unity 3.x Game Development Essentials

ISBN: 978-1-849691-44-4   Paperback: 488 pages

Build fully functional, professional 3D games with realistic environments sound, dynamic effects, and more!

1. Kick start your game development, and build ready-to-play 3D games with ease.

2. Understand key concepts in game design including scripting, physics, instantiation, particle effects, and more.

3. Test & optimize your game to perfection with essential tips-and-tricks.

4. Written in clear, plain English, this book takes you from a simple prototype through to a complete 3D game with concepts you'll reuse throughout your new career as a game developer.

Please check **www.PacktPub.com** for information on our titles

open source*
community experience distilled

Unity iOS Game Development Beginners Guide

ISBN: 978-1-84969-040-9   Paperback: 314 pages

Develop iOS games from concept to cash flow using Unity

1. Dive straight into game development with no previous Unity or iOS experience

2. Work through the entire lifecycle of developing games for iOS

3. Add multiplayer, input controls, debugging, in app and micro payments to your game

4. Implement the different business models that will enable you to make money on iOS games

Unity 3D Game Development by Example Beginner's Guide

ISBN: 978-1-84969-054-6   Paperback: 384 pages

A seat-of-your-pants manual for building fun, groovy little games quickly

1. Build fun games using the free Unity 3D game engine even if you've never coded before

2. Learn how to "skin" projects to make totally different games from the same file – more games, less effort!

3. Deploy your games to the Internet so that your friends and family can play them

4. Packed with ideas, inspiration, and advice for your own game design and development

Please check **www.PacktPub.com** for information on our titles

CPSIA information can be obtained
at www.ICGtesting.com
Printed in the USA
LVOW03s0406250216

476627LV00013B/117/P